The Song of the Viola

The Song of the Viola

AMANDA ROBIN LARCHER

AMBASSADOR INTERNATIONAL
GREENVILLE, SOUTH CAROLINA & BELFAST, NORTHERN IRELAND

www.ambassador-international.com

The Song of the Viola

ISBN: 978-1-62020-279-1
eISBN: 978-1-62020-382-8

Cover Design & Page Layout by Hannah Nichols
Ebook Conversion by Anna Riebe

AMBASSADOR INTERNATIONAL
Emerald House
427 Wade Hampton Blvd.
Greenville, SC 29609, USA
www.ambassador-international.com

AMBASSADOR BOOKS
The Mount
2 Woodstock Link
Belfast, BT6 8DD, Northern Ireland, UK
www.ambassador-international.com

The colophon is a trademark of Ambassador

DEDICATION

To Lauren,

In memory of her beloved brother, Steven Gregory.

The wind blows wherever it pleases
Second Season

CONTENTS

SCIENCE AND LITERATURE

THE TOWN OF LA SERPE is fifteen minutes away from Thym by car, if one crosses the fields. The high school that serves the whole region is there. As for Thym, it is such a small village and the academic level here is so low that very few students, if any, make it to high school. If they do, they have to spend a whole hour on the bus to go to La Serpe as well as to return, for the bus does not cut straight through the fields but circles around to pick up the riders with monthly bus passes who are commuting to town every day.

Amanda was entering seconde[1], in the science section. Her father, Armand Vissac, had just found a good job in La Serpe as a bus driver. It was time for the Vissac family to leave Thym. They took advantage of the vacation of the summer of 1977 to move to La Serpe, to what was called la Cité Américaine, a neighborhood of individual houses surrounded by lawns.

* * *

One afternoon, about a month after school had started again, Amanda sat in her French class. The class had just begun and the

[1]Tenth grade

teacher, M. Mansous, was talking endlessly as usual. "Today, I'm going to give you back your first French homework of the year. I must say that I have been pleasantly surprised to discover that one of you in this class has a real talent in literature. In a science-oriented class, it is rare if it exists at all. This person, and I'm not going to give you her name, simply wrote a perfect paper. It is exactly a model of what I was expecting. Therefore, I'm going to read it to you. Of course, the person will recognize herself—but just listen, all of you, very carefully. It is worth it!"

After such an introduction, the whole class was holding its breath, wondering who could have written the wonderful paper. M. Mansous began. "Imagination. Imagination, as we present it today, is useful only in some artistic professions, but everywhere else it is considered good for nothing else except to make us dream. However, imagination is what allows us to penetrate reality the best.

"Man without imagination is a limited being and consequently not favorable to progress. Scientific inventions need imagination to progress. Man without imagination is not capable of putting himself in his neighbor's place often because of strict reasoning. Sensibility suffers the most from the lack of imagination, because it leads to the lack of understanding of the other . . ."

As he was reading, Amanda could feel the red creep up her cheeks. After the teacher was finished, he slid the paper back in the middle of the others and started to distribute the corrected homework to his students, commenting on it along the way. When he stopped in front of the young lady, he quickly handed the paper to her and said, "Bravo!"

Her neighbor, behind her back, bent forward to glance over her shoulder. She could clearly see the A at the top of the paper. The news spread around the room like wildfire. The next highest mark was a C.

* * *

Science class was different. Mme Riguet was the main teacher of Amanda's tenth-grade class. She taught physics and chemistry. She talked very fast and very low. That day, Amanda found a place on the second row from the front. As soon as Mme Riguet started her lecture, Amanda raised her hand: "Excusez moi, madame! Could you speak louder? I can't hear what you're saying."

Mme Riguet went on with the lesson. Amanda put her hand up again. "Pardon, madame! Could you please slow down? I don't have enough time to write down my notes."

"Well then, I'm going to write on the board!" Mme Riguet offered.

She started to write furiously on the board, but all the time she was writing, she was standing right in front of the text. Amanda tried to twist in every way she possibly could but she only managed to get the beginnings or the ends of a few sentences. Mme Riguet was coming to the bottom of the board. Amanda was starting to hope that she could finally fill in her blanks when her teacher erased the whole thing.

"Please, non!" Amanda protested.

Mme Riguet turned around and looked at her reproachfully. No one else had the gumption to complain. She began to write a few more lines, erased them as fast as the first ones, and then went back to her spoken lesson in a low voice. Discouraged, Amanda sighed and dropped her pen on her desk.

After the session ended, the students started for a study room that was situated under the roof of an older building. Amanda sat down at a desk, pulled her chemistry notebook out of her bag, meditated on it for a minute, and then got up. She walked up to Karine, determined. Karine was the best in the class on this subject.

"Karine, please, would you lend me your notes on the last chemistry lesson? I didn't manage to write even half of it."

Karine wavered. "I don't like to lend my notes!"

"S'il te plaît, just this one time! I'll give it back to you right away."

The student handed her a sheet of paper.

"Thanks, it's very kind of you. I'm going to copy it right now, and I'll return it to you."

Delighted, Amanda went back to her seat. She was about to copy the notes when she stopped short, her pen up, perplexed. The paper had even less information than hers. All she could see on it were three lines of an illegible handwritten script. She got up. Karine was talking with two of her friends. She looked up. "You're done?"

"Uh . . . I'm not sure," Amanda answered. "What I want is the paper with the lesson of today."

Karine grabbed her paper back: "This is the lesson!"

Amanda was embarrassed. "Well then . . . Tell me how you are able to be the best student in the class in chemistry with only that!"

Karine shrugged, slipped the paper into her bag and, without paying any more attention to Amanda, went back to talking to her friends. Amanda hesitated and then slowly walked back to her place. She put away her chemistry notebook.

STRIKE DAY

A FEW DAYS LATER, AMANDA was heading toward her class when Emma, her best friend, came to meet her. "Bonjour, Amanda!"

"Salut!"

As they passed by the covered playground, they noticed a crowd. The covered playground had one open side. Actually it was not used as a playground, but rather as a shelter against the rain. However, today was different. It wasn't raining. "What's going on here?"

"We have decided to go on strike."

"Who do you mean by we?"

"The students and the teachers. Want to be a part of it?"

"It all depends . . ." Amanda answered.

"It's about the new laws that the Assembly is planning to enact. You know, the laws about school policy in—"

"I don't care about that for one minute," Amanda interrupted.

"Well, it all depends on what, then?"

"Just on the weather! If it's sunny, I'd rather spend the day outside."

Karine was one of the leaders. She held onto a microphone, and she kept it for the rest of the day, while the high school crowd marched through the city of La Serpe, in the beautiful sunshine.

* * *

In the afternoon, Amanda went back home. She pulled her bicycle out of the shed and hurried to Simone's health food store.

"Hi, Simone!" She went around the counter to greet her, kissing her first on the left cheek, then on the right.

Simone was in her fifties. Her face was framed by salt-and-pepper hair, but her beauty remained untouched.

"It's deadly quiet here today."

"That's right. I haven't seen many customers so far. I think I'm going to close early."

Amanda smiled. "Good. That way we can talk!"

Simone sighed: "Good for you, but not for my business!"

The girl didn't reply. She was meandering around the shop that she knew by heart.

"Okay, what do you want to discuss?"

"Frankly, I find the plight of the few Christians of La Serpe to be deplorable," Amanda started.

"Really? What makes you think so?"

"On one side of town lives a pastor who has no meeting place and hence no congregation, and in another neighborhood there are a few Christians who have a meeting place but no pastor. And the two just never meet together."

"It's more complicated than that," Simone answered wisely. "Behind this lies the question of secondary beliefs."

"And of labels," her young friend added.

"Yes, of denominational labels!"

"Here is the choice I'm faced with: to meet alone with the pastor or to join the few Christians who meet together."

"Well, which are you going to choose?"

"The brothers and sisters! I'm tired of being isolated with my faith. Besides, the pastor should be smart enough to understand that."

Simone shrugged. "You would think so."

"Meanwhile, I'm starving spiritually."

"Well, dear, that's your choice."

"And what about you? What are you going to do?"

"I'm going to try to maintain a good relationship with everyone. But I think I might as well join you."

Amanda's face brightened.

"What I miss the most here is witnessing!" Simone went on. "Nothing is organized."

"What would you like to do exactly?"

"Go out into the streets, for instance. But in order to do that, it's best to do it with at least one other person."

"Why can't we do it then? We could go out, the two of us, you and me. You know how it works; I'll keep you company, and you show me how to do it."

"You'd come with me? That would be wonderful!"

"When do we start?"

"Tonight! The weather is beautiful, and I wanted to close early anyway. We'll pass by my house to collect some tracts, and we'll distribute them in the cafés."

* * *

Two hours later, the two ladies were finishing their round of the downtown cafés of La Serpe. The people sitting inside and out had politely accepted the tracts. The sun was slowly setting in the sky.

Simone offered her tracts to some people on the street as well. She sighed. "One more café! I'm exhausted."

"I'll go by myself!"

"Sure. You know the approach now. It's not that difficult. I'll wait for you outside. Meanwhile, I'll distribute my tracts to the passersby."

Amanda entered a dark lair. A strong smell of alcohol and cigarette smoke filled the air. She felt uncomfortable but walked up to the back of the room, distributing her little papers along the way. At the last table, she stopped, surprised. Karine's thick hair was casting a light glow in the darkness.

"Hi!" Amanda said, handing her a tract.

Karine didn't answer. She took the paper and glanced at it while her schoolmate was waiting for her greeting. Suddenly, Karine sat up and spat on the floor. "Christians!" Her face was full of contempt. She threw the paper at Amanda's face, who watched it helplessly flutter to the ground. She picked it up though and slowly backed toward the entry. The light of the day and the presence of Simone reassured her.

"So?" her older friend asked.

Amanda breathed in the gentle evening breeze. "I was just properly sent back into my shoes by a classmate."

"That's part of witnessing. You are becoming a pro!"

A MISTAKE

THE END OF THE FIRST school term was fast approaching, and the class councils had just come to the closing stages. The next day, Mlle Verges, the high school math teacher, finished her lecture, and then called, "Amanda! Could you spare me a minute, please? I would like to talk to you."

"Oui, mademoiselle."

Amanda came to the teacher's desk and waited while she was erasing the board. Mlle Verges finally turned to her and began with her soft voice, saying, "We just finished the class councils. Your average in math is not very good."

"Neither is it in the other scientific subjects," Amanda remarked.

"Probably, but the other scientific subjects are not my responsibility."

Her student kept quiet.

"You are a serious student and I believe intelligent, so it bothers me to see that you have some obvious difficulties in math. I would like to help you, but I don't know exactly how."

"That's very kind of you, mademoiselle, but your courses are perfect, and I don't see what else you could do."

"Then why do you average only ten out of twenty?"

"There are some things I don't understand; I can't tell exactly why. However, when you explain, they all seem clear to me—but then I can't reproduce them."

"This makes me think you could do it. In my opinion, you are lacking in some fundamentals. You need to find a good ninth-grade book of math and read through it."

Amanda sighed. "Oui, mademoiselle. You are probably right."

"Well then, don't give up now. It's too early in the school year yet. Rather: good luck!"

"Thank you!" Amanda smiled at her. Mlle Verges was so sweet.

* * *

Amanda caught up with her classmates. M. Mansous hadn't arrived yet, and they were waiting in front of the door of the French class. The entrance to the classroom was situated in a nook around the corner of a wall.

As soon as Véronique saw Amanda come in, she straightened the whole length of her short body and turned her mouse-like keen face toward her. "M. Mansous is going to give us our papers today!"

"I hate French!" Karine remarked.

"Just guess who's going to get the highest mark," Véronique's low-pitched voice went on.

They all looked at Amanda.

"Well, la chouchoute,[2] bien sûr!" Véronique announced triumphantly.

A few laughs burst out. Amanda stood to the side, determined to ignore her, but the girl came up to her and shook her finger under

---

[2]Chouchoute: teacher's pet.

her nose. "Yes, yes! She is the teacher's pet," she insisted. "Haven't you noticed? Amanda here, Amanda there! I'm starting to think that old Mansous is losing his mind. He only cares for her. I bet that she's still going to get an A or something like that—right? What do you say about this, teacher's pet?"

"You talk too much, Véronique," Amanda answered calmly. "Do you truly believe that he's marking my work just for the sake of my pretty eyes?"

"Absolutely!" Véronique looked at her with utter disgust. "Chouchoute!"

At that very moment M. Mansous stepped around the corner. He glanced at the two students facing each other but unlocked the door without a word. He probably heard the last sentences.

* * *

At the end of the class, M. Mansous called Amanda to his desk. Véronique, curious, was dragging her feet. Amanda was definitely getting a lot of attention from their teachers today.

"Everybody else out!" he ordered.

However, he left the door open while Emma discreetly waited for her friend in the corridor. Once alone with the young lady, he asked, "Amanda, are you happy in this class?"

"I have a hard time with the antagonism."

"What do you mean?"

"Well . . . there is no solidarity. Sometimes when I ask for help, I get the impression that the best students wouldn't even tell me that one plus one equals two—for fear that I might receive a higher mark than they do. However, I'm no danger to them."

Mansous thought silently for a few seconds. "There is one thing I don't understand: how did you end up in a science-oriented curriculum?"

Amanda nodded. "I've come from a little country school, monsieur. We didn't have any choices for our foreign languages other than English—mandatory as a first language—and German as a second. From there, I think they directed most of their best students into science classes. You see, we weren't that many, and the reputation of the school is important."

M. Mansous shook his head. "This is a major mistake. You are literary, and you've been placed in the wrong class."

Amanda looked at him attentively, waiting for more.

"Well, good evening!" he said sharply. He grabbed his briefcase and walked away while Amanda stood there, glued to her spot. Emma stuck her head through the doorway. "Are you coming? It's late!"

"I wonder what he was trying to tell me."

Emma stepped into the room and pulled Amanda's sleeve. "You're not going to find out by staying here!"

Amanda sighed and followed her friend.

GOOD AND EVIL

THE CHRISTMAS VACATION HAD PASSED. The weather had turned cold and damp. The second trimester had started. Emma and Amanda, wrapped up in their warmest coats, were walking past the school's covered playground when they noticed a little group that had formed there around Karine.

"Would you like to become a member of the French communist party?" Emma asked her friend.

"No, thanks! I'm not interested in that. But why are you asking me this question?"

"They are offering cards of the party," she answered, pointing to the gathering.

"What about you? Did you purchase one?"

"I didn't. You know, politics is not my thing. Later on, I hope to become a chiropractor. It is the best profession in the whole wide world. And you, what do you plan to be later?"

"I don't know yet, but come! Let's listen to what she is saying."

Karine was making a speech. The two friends drew closer.

The speaker noticed Amanda right away. "Communism is the future of our country. We are living in a revolutionary time in which we have finally recognized that there is no future in holding onto the old-fashioned, outdated beliefs of the Judeo-Christian society of yesterday."

She stared at Amanda. "In fact, who in our time could still support the idea that values such as good and evil exist? I am challenging anyone who has a brain to define for me good and evil, those two great concepts of Christianity. On what basis do we have the right to say that one thing is good and another is evil?"

As Amanda was listening, her mouth opened. Emma pulled her away. "Come on, let's go. What she is promoting is of no interest."

Amanda followed her. She was embarrassed. "You may be right, Emma. Except that she was aiming straight at me!"

"What do you mean?"

"Did you hear what she said?"

"I did. I think it was rather stupid!"

"Perhaps . . . but would you know how to answer her?"

Emma shrugged. "Do I have to?"

* * *

Back at home, that evening, Armand and his wife Louise exchanged news of the day at the supper table while Amanda was lost in her thoughts. Then Armand turned to his daughter. "And what about you, ma chérie, did you have a good day?"

"Papa, I have a puzzling question for you."

"Go ahead!"

"What would you say to someone who doesn't believe in the existence of good and evil?"

"Why are you asking me this question?"

"It's because of Karine, a girl in my class. She pretends there's no distinction between good and evil. She challenged everyone, and me in particular, to prove to her there's a difference between good and evil."

"Well then, what do you think?"

"It seems so obvious to me there's good and evil . . ."

"Good for you!"

"Yes, but it's so obvious that I have no idea how to explain it. Why . . . it's just as clear as day!"

"I agree with you. And the real problem is that, because she got to you so effectively, she'll keep coming back to it, using the same argument each time she wants to put you down."

"I'm afraid of that!"

"But it also gives you an advantage. You'll get your chance to answer her back. Just be ready for it!"

"How? What can I say to her?"

"Nothing!" Her father answered mischievously.

"Come on, Papa, what would you do in my place?"

"Well . . . next time she provokes you, slap her on the face!" he answered seriously.

"Papa!" she protested.

"Oh yes, I'll allow you! Then you can ask her if it would have been any different if you had kissed her instead."

Amanda burst out laughing. "Papa, you are great! The only problem is that I'm totally unable to slap anyone on the face."

Armand smiled. "You've got the idea, however. I trust you. You'll find a solution."

* * *

"Amanda!" It was during one of those long and boring recesses.

Amanda turned around. Cédric was waving at her in the distance. A young lady accompanied him, and they were walking toward her. "Good morning!"

"I want to introduce Émilie to you. She wanted to meet you," Cédric said.

Émilie wasn't very pretty, but she had the most charming smile. "Good morning, Amanda. Can you spare a minute? I'd like to talk to you."

"Yes, sure," Amanda answered, surprised.

"First of all, let me introduce myself. I'm a pianist, and I study under Madame Geneviève d'Autan. She is in the process of building a semi-professional orchestra. Cédric is part of it already. He plays the first violin solo. Geneviève is looking for some additional second violins. Cédric told me that at the music school, you come right after him. She could surely use you. What do you think?"

"I don't know," Amanda answered cautiously. "I would need to ask my parents first and then meet with her. I'm not sure I'm good enough."

"You must absolutely meet with her, then. You'll see; she has a heart. Besides, you should know she holds a 'First Prize of Rome.'"

"So what do you think?" Amanda asked Cédric.

He shrugged. "If I were you, I'd give it a try. It can't hurt."

"If my parents agree, what should I do then?"

"Come to the next rehearsal. It's at her place in the country. I'm going to give you her address right away and the next rehearsal dates."

Émilie, excited, was getting some notepaper out of her bag.

"You really think I can show up just like that?"

"Of course you can. She's expecting you. She really hopes you will come!"

Amanda smiled. "Well then, I'm sure it's all right!"

Émilie hugged her warmly. "Wonderful!"

* * *

"Amanda, wait for me!" Emma, out of breath, was coming her way. As the two young ladies walked away, they passed by the covered playground. Amanda stopped. "Look there! Karine is giving another of her recruiting talks," she remarked.

Emma pulled her by the arm. "Come on, let's go or she's going to provoke you again."

Amanda gently freed herself. "No, Emma. Just wait for me here. I want to hear what she has to say today."

As soon as Karine noticed her, her speech switched to a challenge against traditional values. Her girlfriends watched Amanda draw closer with sarcastic smiles. Quickly, Karine moved on to her favorite subject. "Those who still believe it is possible to determine values such as good and evil are really living in a prehistoric world. I haven't yet met with anyone who could prove me wrong on that."

While Emma was prudently keeping her distance, Amanda drew a deep breath and moved forward, determined. "I'm willing to try to prove you wrong on that one!" she defied.

"All right! Go ahead!"

Amanda took her time. She pushed her way forward between the girls, forcing the heavy winter coats to make space to let her through. Karine impatiently said, "I'm waiting!"

"It's all right, just wait!"

While Karine was growing ill at ease, Amanda walked up to her until they were face to face.

She smiled her brightest smile. "Hey! We haven't greeted yet!"

She came close and kissed Karine on both cheeks. The young communist froze. "Your arguments?"

Amanda took one step backward. "You are lucky I'm in a good mood today!" she answered calmly, but loud enough for everyone to hear. "I could have slapped you right across the face to greet you . . . for as you maintain, it doesn't make any difference."

Karine opened her mouth, but no sound came out of it. Amanda sauntered away, leaving a thick silence behind her. This time, she had no trouble clearing her way through the coats. The girls respectfully stepped backward to let her through. Amanda rejoined Emma. "I think that from now on, she'll leave me alone."

Emma didn't answer but under her white woolen hat from which blonde locks escaped, she smiled widely—proud of her friend.

NEW ORIENTATION

OUTSIDE, SPRINGTIME WAS FAST APPROACHING. Like every Tuesday evening, in the big auditorium of the music school, Amanda pulled her violin out of its case. Cédric came in.

"Hi, Cédric! Tell me, did you receive the same letter that I did?"

The young musician pulled an envelope out of the inner pocket of his vest. "This?" He pulled a letter out of the envelope and started to read aloud: "Any student of the Township Music School of La Serpe wishing to participate in an orchestra outside of this same music school must first request authorization from the director, or he will be stricken from the roll."

Amanda frowned and glanced over his shoulder to see the words. "That's it! Do you understand what it means?"

"Well, it's obvious, isn't it?"

"Who does the word director refer to?"

"Antoine Marcelin, of course!"

"Aïe! We are already playing in another orchestra."

"Yes, and to tell you the truth, you and I are the only ones this letter relates to in this whole school."

"You really think we are going to be removed from the roll?"

"No, I don't think so. Actually, this is my fault. I haven't been coming regularly to the rehearsals here. I find it so boring."

"I've noticed. Each time you are absent, I have to take your place. But you are the best, and we need you."

Cédric sighed and pulled his instrument out of its box. "I'm finishing twelfth grade this year, and I'm going to the Conservatoire de Versailles. I can't do it all!" He began to tune his violin.

"Why do you still come here, then?"

"Because of the violin teacher. But you know, you're going to start getting bored here too. You should think of going to Versailles also."

"You think so?"

"Why not? It would be good for you!"

"Well, meanwhile, what should we do? Are you going to write to ask for an authorization to play in Madame d'Autan's orchestra?"

Cédric stuck his violin under his arm. "I won't. Just leave it to me. As soon as Monsieur Marcelin comes in, I'm going to ask him for the authorization, for you and for me."

"Thanks, that's kind of you but . . . aren't you afraid he's going to get upset at you?"

Cédric smiled. "We never know with him. However, if he wants me to stay, he'll behave decently."

Just then, Antoine Marcelin walked in. Cédric braced himself and put his violin down. "Let's go!"

Amanda followed him.

"Good afternoon, Monsieur Marcelin!"

The director shook their hands.

"We've received a letter from you. I'd like to ask you for permission to play in Madame d'Autan's orchestra, for me and Amanda too."

"I don't have anything against it," the director answered quietly. "However, there's one condition, and this is especially for you, Cédric: I don't want to see you miss the rehearsals of this orchestra anymore."

Cédric nodded. Antoine Marcelin went on. "Besides, I've just discovered a lovely musical piece for two violins soli with string accompaniment. I would like for you and Amanda to play it. I hope you'll like it. Come on, let's get to work!"

The two young violinists exchanged a glance of relief and went to their seats next to each other. M. Marcelin started by making the youngest ensemble rehearse. Cédric began to yawn. The conductor was loudly beating the rhythm on the head of the music stand, which was slowly declining toward the ground. Cédric hid behind his instrument to smile and then discreetly pulled a soft caramel out of his pocket. He handed it to Amanda. She seized it and slid it in her pocket. He took out another caramel and, despite the horrified look of his friend, quickly unwrapped it (while the string instruments were covering the noise of the paper) and shoved it into his mouth. At the same instant, M. Marcelin ordered, "Everybody, together!"

The two first violinists tucked their instrument under their chins. The conductor gave the starting signal. Cédric had a habit of playing with his mouth open, so he tried to open his jaws—but they remained glued to one another. He gave Amanda a desperate look. She could hardly refrain from laughter. Fortunately, they had to stop, for the other violinists were not quite ready.

* * *

Amanda's report card for the second school trimester arrived in the mail. Louise examined it and sighed. "Your marks in science and math haven't been going up, Amanda."

"I'd even say they've been going down," her daughter remarked realistically.

"How come?"

"In physics and chemistry, the explanation is easy. The teacher's voice is inaudible, and what she writes on the board is invisible. I stopped taking notes a long time ago. I wonder how the other students do it, but they seem to be making out."

"I suspect they have some help at home."

"Or they are gifted."

"That's possible also."

"With math, it's another story. The teacher is perfect, but she said I was lacking in some fundamentals. She wished I'd go back to a ninth-grade program, but I don't know where to find that."

"Why didn't you tell me? Of course you need some books. If you want, we'll go to the bookstore together. We'll check into what they have."

"No, I don't want any book!"

"Why not?"

"If the courses aren't good enough—too bad! I don't want to spend all of my free time reading math and science."

"You are stubborn!"

"Monsieur Mansous said I was literary!"

"He's right," Armand stepped in. "I don't see what you are doing in a scientific program."

"Cédric advised me to try to enter the Conservatoire de Versailles next September. If I continue in the sciences, I'll never be able to do everything."

"It's a good idea," Louise approved. "I'm not against it, but it's going to be difficult. I don't know if they're going to let you move from a science emphasis to a literary one."

"To go from literature into the sciences is almost impossible, but as to the other way around, I've heard of a few exceptions. Then there's Monsieur Mansous. He's a good man and respected. I'm going to talk to him."

Armand smiled, relieved. "You have my full support. I think your place is in a literary program."

* * *

As soon as the French class was over, M. Mansous stepped out in a hurry. Amanda ran after him. "Monsieur Mansous!"

He turned around. "What do you want?"

"I'd like to talk to you. Can you spare a minute?"

"Go ahead. I'm listening."

"I'd like to move over to a literary track. Could you help me?"

M. Mansous stopped entirely, looked at her, and rubbed his chin with his hand, thoughtful. "Well . . . It's not as simple as that," he finally answered.

He read disappointment in her eyes. "Wait! Let me explain to you! In this school, there are two literary tracks. One of the two is not truly a literary program. It's a class where those who can't do anything else go. Forgive me the word, but I'd call it the trash of the school. In the other group are the true literary students. However,

Latin or Greek is an absolute minimum requirement to enter it. Do you understand that?"

"Oui, monsieur."

M. Mansous went on gently. "If I fight for you to enter the literary track—for you must not dream, we'll have to fight—I don't want you to fall into the school's trash barrel."

As Amanda was drinking in each of his words, hope was slowly returning to her face.

"I'm willing to fight for you," he continued. "You're worth it; but I have one condition." He paused.

"What is it?"

"That you learn Latin or Greek!"

Amanda grinned. "D'accord, monsieur, I'll learn anything you want!"

"I know a young lady. Her name is Émilie. She is in twelfth grade, and she is excellent in Latin. I heard she wants to become a teacher. I'll ask her to contact you. I think she'll be very happy to help."

"Would you mean Émilie Jonquin?"

"You know her?"

"Yes, I do. She is a musician like me."

"Are you?"

"Yes, I am. I play the violin. Come September, I'd like to apply to enter the Conservatoire de Versailles."

"Well, I'm beginning to understand. I'm putting the pieces of the puzzle together. I'll let you contact her directly then, but I'll make sure I talk to her too. I know her father well. He's one of the medical doctors of the school. Now, as far as I'm concerned, you can count on me; I'll do my best. However . . ."

"Yes?"

"I hope you understand everything does not depend on me. You know Madame Riguet. She's not easy, and she seems rather determined to see you through another year of tenth-grade science. Don't forget she's your main teacher. Her opinion carries more weight than mine in the decision-making process concerning your orientation. If I don't get the support of Mademoiselle Verges, I don't know what's going to happen."

"She's a sweetheart!"

"Yes, but unfortunately she thinks you're smart, and she'd like to see you stay in the scientific section too. Scientists have a tendency to think that one can't be smart and literary at the same time. Anyway, nothing is sure yet."

"I'll pray for that," Amanda concluded with serenity.

Her old teacher stared at her, surprised. Embarrassed, she quickly said, "Good-bye, Monsieur Mansous, and thank you for everything!"

M. Mansous watched Amanda walk away, sighed, and shook his head.

CONCERTS AND ANGELS

THE COUNCIL FOR AMANDA'S TENTH-GRADE class was meeting. Mme Riguet was going down the roll of the students without too much difficulty.

"Joël Norman: Pass.

"Amanda Vissac: Fail."

M. Mansous looked up. "I'm requesting that she be transferred to the eleventh-grade literature class."

"You can't be serious!"

"Yes, I am. I spoke with the young lady, and she would like to go into literature."

"She's a smart kid. We can't let her go into L2."

"I agree with you. I'm asking for her to go into L1."

"This is impossible. She has only two foreign languages."

"She'll learn Latin."

"Catch up with three years of Latin? This is ridiculous!"

"I wonder why she chose a scientific section to start with?" Mlle Verges interjected with her soft voice.

"She didn't really choose. She has been ill oriented, that's all. You already know my opinion about her. She truly belongs to the literature world. Her place is not in sciences."

Mlle Verges blinked. There was a silence.

"I propose flunked," Mme Riguet insisted.

"I oppose it," M. Mansous answered.

The student representative—attending on behalf of her classmates and listening to that exchange—was startled, as if watching a table tennis match. All the heads turned to Mlle Verges. She asked, "What would this young lady like to do with her life?"

"She wants to be a musician. In September, she will apply for entrance at the Conservatoire de Versailles."

"She is an artist!" the English teacher exclaimed.

"She is a violinist," M. Mansous specified.

"Well then . . . in that case . . . I think it might be better, indeed, for her to move to a literary track," Mlle Verges finally concluded.

"Who agrees to the proposal to transfer Amanda Vissac to literature?" Mme Riguet asked.

A majority of hands rose up. She sighed.

⋆ ⋆ ⋆

The next day when Amanda arrived at the school, the president of the students of her class stopped her on her way. "Hi, Amanda! Do you know how lucky you are?"

"No, why?"

"Boy, was it hot yesterday at our class council—all because of you! I've never seen anything like it before. I wish you could have seen Monsieur Mansous. He supported you to death against Riguet."

"So what happened?"

Her schoolmate didn't have time to answer.

"Amanda!"

The old French teacher, at the end of the passage, waved widely to them. "Amanda! We won!" he yelled.

The students who were going to their classes stopped on their way to stare at them. They let the man walk through them like a tornado. The students' president smiled and stepped back. "I'll let him break the news to you!"

M. Mansous caught up with them. "It's a complete victory!" he declared, out of breath. "You pass en première[3] L1!"

Amanda—with a grateful smile—held her hand out. The old man took her hand and shook it.

* * *

That evening, the weather was deliciously warm, and Louise invited Amanda to join her on a walk. They headed for the center of the town which, at this time of the year, was lively with early summer shoppers. For the first time in their lives, mother and daughter stopped in front of an old-fashioned tearoom downtown. The little French pastries looked so inviting.

"Would you like to go in?" Louise suggested. "We'll order something sweet and sit down."

"Oh, oui!"

They found a table in a cool and quiet corner.

"Another concert has gone by," Amanda sighed.

---

[3]Eleventh grade

"Yes, your duet with Cédric was lovely, and you were so pretty in your long velvet skirt and white shirt."

"Oh, Maman, you always think I'm pretty," Amanda protested.

"I was proud of you, and so was Papa." Her mother smiled. "We weren't the only ones to find you pretty either. So did Cédric's parents."

"How do you know this?"

Louise giggled joyfully. "You know how Cédric opens his mouth when he plays. Well, at the end of the concert, Papa told his father, 'Say, your son is a splendid violinist! But what a grin . . .' Monsieur Aubray said, 'I know! Your daughter was so much more gracious!'"

Amanda was delighted. "Is that right? That's not very kind about his son."

"I believe they really like you. What about you? What do you think of Cédric?"

"He's gifted, and he's a hard worker."

"You know, there's nothing wrong with being friends with him. He wants to be a musician, and so do you . . ."

Amanda wavered before answering. "I know, but he isn't really my type."

"What's your type?"

"A born-again Christian. I doubt that faith is one of his pursuits."

"I'm sure his parents are good practicing Catholics."

"Probably, but this is not sufficient for me."

"How do you know the extent of his belief in God?"

"I don't know. He's serious. But I doubt that he's a Christian the way I understand it."

Her mother sighed. "Anyway, you'll see. You're still young."

"I sure am."

A waiter brought the ice cream they had ordered.

"Meanwhile, fifteen more days and we're going to play the Fortieth and Coriolan at the music hall," the young violinist went on.

"It's going to be different."

"Yes, it's much more work—and I'm only second violin. I'm going to long for our little orchestra where I played as a star."

"It'll be good all the same," her mother assured her. "You'll have an opportunity to play with professionals."

Amanda laughed. "To tell the truth, I can't wait!"

★ ★ ★

School was over. The office was still processing the files of the students. Émilie Jonquin stuck her head in the door. "Is my father somewhere around here?"

"No, honey! And you, what are you doing here?"

Émilie stepped into the office. "I just came by to kiss you because you're so sweet!"

"And you're just a big heart."

The secretary looked up from the files. Émilie went around the desk and kissed her; then she backed up and laid a hand on a file that was on the top of one of the piles. "Would you like some help, Madame Merle?"

"No, thank you! It's very kind of you but all this has to pass by me."

Without thinking, the young lady glanced at the file that was right under her hand. A thick red line crossed it through. "Amanda Vissac," she slowly read. "But I know her!"

"Oh, yes! That Amanda Vissac!" Mme Merle burst out. "Well, I can tell you that her file bothers me. I don't know what to do with it. She wants to pass to eleventh grade L1, with Latin—and she never had any Latin. This cannot work. It just can't work at all. Besides, her main teacher told me she thought it would be better for her to flunk—"

"Don't get so upset, Madame Merle. I know her. She's very serious, and she's already started to catch up with Latin."

"Just like that? All by herself?"

"No, of course not. She has a teacher. Actually, I happen to know her teacher as well. I can assure you she's got an excellent teacher." Émilie was smiling mischievously.

"Really?"

"It's as I'm telling you! Would you ever doubt my word, Madame Merle?"

"But no! Not you!"

"Well then, do you see this file? Just nicely put it on the pile of the eleventh grade L1 and you won't have any more trouble with it. That's one less big problem for you."

The secretary took the file, wavered one second, and placed it on the pile of the eleventh grade L1.

⋆ ⋆ ⋆

On a mild and quiet summer evening, Amanda arrived at Émilie's. She found the door of the ancient mansion wide open. Émilie was at the piano, waiting for her. She was playing the famous "Fur Elise." Amanda discreetly entered the wide, cool living room, furnished in an old-fashioned style. A smell of fresh wax emanated from the old furniture, which was glowing with warm and friendly reflections. She waited for her friend to stop playing to greet her.

"Amanda! Would you play some music with me?"

"I'm sorry, Émilie, but I don't have any spare time left. Besides Latin, I've started to work in a children's day camp to be able to pay for the Conservatoire."

Émilie was smiling. "Well, Amanda, I can tell God is with you."

"I believe so. But why are you saying that?"

"Let me tell you what happened to me this morning."

When Émilie came to the part where she had "praised" the Latin teacher, she burst out laughing, until tears ran down her cheeks. She finally managed to catch her breath. "I told her you had an excellent Latin teacher. She never knew I was talking about me."

Amanda declared very seriously, "But it's true; you're really good."

Émilie wiped her eyes. Amanda went on. "So, you believe in God."

"Yes, I do."

Amanda looked at her fondly and softly said, "Well, I also believe He put some angels along my path."

Émilie melted. "Oh, Amanda!" she exclaimed.

THE VIOLIST

AMANDA ENTERED ELEVENTH GRADE IN the literary track. She also took the violin entry exam at the Conservatoire Régional de Musique de Versailles. She waited for the results and drew a deep breath to gather her courage; then she went to knock at the door of the office of the Conservatoire.

"Come in!"

"Good afternoon, madame. Excuse me for bothering you. I've just taken the violin entry exam for the middle class[1], and I don't see my name on the admission list. So I would like to know the reason for me being refused."

The lady sighed. "Why would you want to know the reason?"

"I'd like to know if I could try again next year."

"Wait a minute." The lady got up and drew a file out of a metal organizer. "What's your name?"

"Amanda Vissac."

"Yes, here you are. What's your age?"

"I'm sixteen."

"You are one year too old for the level. No, there is no need for you to come back next year. You see, we have three violin classes of thirty students each, and we don't know where to put them anymore."

"Thank you, madame." Her throat tight, Amanda left the Conservatoire behind her. The wind was blowing the dead leaves of the old platanes[4] in circles toward the gates of King Louis the Fourteenth's famous castle. She headed in the opposite direction, toward the train station.

* * *

After one hour on the train, Amanda arrived at La Serpe. Her violin case strapped on her shoulder, she walked down the wide avenue, passed through downtown, entered a narrow road that climbed up sharply, and finally arrived at her home at the top of the hill. When she pushed the door open, Louise appeared at the kitchen doorframe. Armand was sitting at the dining room table. He looked up from the paper he was reading. The young violinist closed the door, stopped, and sighed.

"Well, chérie?" her father asked softly.

"I've been refused."

"Maybe you can try again next year?"

"No, I'm too old for the level."

She just stood there, looking at the sorry faces of her parents. Suddenly, she left the living room and headed for her bedroom. "For me, it's the end of my musical career," she pronounced with a broken voice. She drew the door behind her, threw herself on her bed, and

[4]Platane: A popular shade tree, with broad leaves and bi-colored bark, lining roads and public squares across France.

started to sob the tears of despair she had been holding back all the way home.

Armand got up. He quietly pushed open the door that wasn't locked and stepped into his daughter's room. He sat on the bed next to her and gently pulled her against him. It seemed impossible to comfort her, so he didn't say anything. She cried for a long time; he didn't move. He kept holding her face tenderly against his chest. Amanda felt the warmth of the sweater, the security of the masculine muscles against her cheek. Little by little, she started to think again. The rhythm of the powerful heartbeats of her father was penetrating her. She calmed down. "All I was hoping for is going up in smoke. My whole life is ruined," she finally managed to utter.

Armand got up. "Not so!" he answered firmly. "Life doesn't stop here and now. In any case, this is not going to keep the earth from turning."

Amanda looked up. Her father was leaving her room. She jumped up and went after him into the living room. "Papa, I've got an idea!"

"Tell us!"

Louise had come out of the kitchen again.

"I know, it's probably stupid, a crazy idea; but there's still one hope. However, I don't know how possible it could be."

"Just say it!" her mother encouraged.

"I heard there's a really good viola teacher in Versailles, and he has very few students. He might still have a place for me."

"How do you know this?"

"Cédric told me."

"Would you like to try?"

"Yes, but I'm afraid it might be too late. The entry exams are over."

"In any case, you wouldn't have been able to present anything with a viola."

"That's right. The music range is different, lower. The clef is different. This might be the reason why fewer students are taking viola than violin. However, it's a beautiful instrument."

"Do you think you'd like it?"

"I think so. The technique has to be pretty close to the one for the violin. The only problem is, I don't have a viola."

"Yes, and it represents a sum of money."

Louise was hesitant. "I'm working, and you are the only one left at home. I must admit that financially we are doing better than we used to. I think that, if Papa agrees and if the viola teacher accepts you, you can count on us for this."

Amanda turned to her father.

"Of course, I agree," Armand approved. "It's worth trying."

"You really think so?"

"What's the big risk?"

"Oh, thank you! Next Wednesday, I'll go back to Versailles!"

* * *

A week later, Amanda entered the courtyard of the Conservatoire. The viola study room was not in the main building, situated at the back of the yard. It was right at the entry, on the right-hand side, and it spread the whole length of the side of the court. She entered the dark room. The low ceiling was resting on columns. Toward the back, under a bare electric lamp bulb, a short man with curly gray hair sat on a high stool. A little girl was struggling through a musical scale on a viola. Another child was putting his little instrument away. The teacher turned toward the mother of the little boy.

"Yes, this is a very good idea. If he's hyperactive, music can only do him good. Who cares what he'll do with it? It's excellent therapy."

The mother and child said good-bye and left. Amanda stood there, politely waiting.

"What do you want?"

"I'd like to speak with you."

"Do you mind waiting till the end of this lesson?"

"Of course not!"

The man turned to his student. "I know this is your third year in the same level, but it's not your fault; you're tone-deaf. In any case, I think you've improved a lot, and I believe you can still improve."

"It's against the rules to take the same class three years in a row," the little girl remarked shyly.

"I know. They didn't want to take you back this year, but I took care of that. I told them if you had to leave, I'd leave also." The man had a little mischievous smile.

Finally, the little girl put her instrument away, and the violist started to close up shop. There were no more students in the room. The child left. Amanda came up to the light.

"I'm sorry! You've been as quiet as a mouse, and I forgot all about you. What do you want?"

Amanda explained bravely. "I took the violin entry exam for the middle class1, but I've been refused. So, I've been wondering if there would be any possibility here, with you—"

"Do you know the reason why you've been refused?"

Amanda looked down to the ground. “Yes. They told me I was one year too old for the level.”

The man turned his back on her. “How old are you?”

“I’m sixteen.”

He slowly turned back to her. “You’re sixteen?”

Amanda blushed. “Oui, monsieur!”

The teasing eyes twinkled. “And they say you are too old?”

At the intonation of his voice, she guessed that he wasn’t expecting an answer. She was just observing him, perplexed.

“Did you bring your instrument?”

“Non, monsieur.”

“Why not?” he grumbled. “How am I going to know what you can do?”

“Well . . . I guess I didn’t have much hope, that’s why.”

Without another word, he turned back to his viola case and opened the box. Out of it, he drew a magnificent instrument, its whole wood surface shining brightly, and handed it to the girl. “Here, play a cord for me, anything. You don’t have to put your fingers on it; you are not used to that range anyway.”

Amanda carefully took hold of the instrument, which was probably worth a small fortune, and stuck it under her chin. The teacher handed her the bow. She chose to try the lowest string—the one she didn’t know yet—the only one that didn’t exist on a violin. She delicately laid the bow on this C-string and slowly pulled it down the whole length. As the bow was running, her eyes were shining, her mouth opened. She had never played such a deep sound. “It sounds like velvet!” she exclaimed.

The teacher stopped her. “That’s enough!”

He quietly put his instrument back in its case. "Come back next week with your own viola and we'll start," he finally said.

Amanda was speechless.

"Well, yes. You'll need an instrument!"

"This is not the problem. I'm wondering . . . I don't know if they'll agree at the office."

He laughed. "Don't worry about that. I'll take care of it. I'll register you myself."

"Thank you so much, monsieur!"

Amanda wished she could hug him. He smiled, happy with himself. "See you next Wednesday, then!"

Amanda left the Conservatoire running faster than the leaves in the wind. She wanted to catch the next train for La Serpe.

LATIN CLASS

THE DESKS OF THE LATIN literary class of the eleventh graders had been arranged in a circle. Mme Sabotier, the teacher, was handing copies back to the students. "Amanda, you have an A. It's excellent."

Gilles raised his hand. "Excusez moi, madame. How can she have such a high mark when she just started Latin?"

"Well, maybe we could ask her," the teacher answered, turning to her.

Amanda grinned. "It's simple. I still have all the grammatical rules fresh in my head, but you probably have forgotten them."

"All right, I'm going to give you a translation for the next time. The Latin text is from Tacite. Don't try to get the book at the school library. I warned the librarian. She won't let it out."

The students sighed. As soon as the class was over, they gathered around Amanda. "Would you do this translation for us?"

"Well, no! Don't push things too far. I hate Latin as much as you do!"

"Why did you take it then?"

"Only for the privilege of being in your class and to have you as friends."

"We're overwhelmed by homework these days," a girl complained.

"We are, and we have one more translation to do!"

The Latin students had long faces. Gilles' face brightened. "I've got an idea. I have a cousin in sciences, in twelfth grade. If only he could get that Tacite book for us!"

"That's great. We could all copy from it and just change some things along the way."

"Who doesn't agree?"

Amanda started laughing. "Gilles! You can copy it first, make some changes, and then you pass your copy to someone else and so on. You know, like in the game of the Arab telephone. I just can't wait to see what it's going to look like at the end."

Once the deal was closed, Claire came up to Amanda. "We could be friends, you and me!"

"Yes, I've noticed that you're often on your own, and me too."

Claire smiled. "You know, I'm a communist."

Amanda's face fell. "Oh!"

"What's wrong? Does it bother you?"

"It doesn't. That is . . . I'm a Christian, and I'm afraid it's going to bother you."

"Not at all! You can well believe whatever you want!"

"All right then, we'll be best friends!"

* * *

As the Vissac family sat around the little kitchen table for supper, Amanda held an envelope in her hand.

She declared, "Monsieur Villemin holds first viola solo at the Opéra de Paris. This year, he has only five students; among them are a tone-deaf girl, a hyperactive child, and me. It's a mystery to me. He's a wonderful man, and there's a need for violists."

"We're happy for you," her father answered, smiling. "And what about eleventh grade L1?"

"It's been going as nicely and smoothly as on wheels! I've had no problems at all, and I've made some good friends in that class."

She waved the letter she was holding. "This is from the local office of the Francas Association. I really appreciate their monthly training weekends and also the fact that it's free of charge. They probably sent invitations to all the supervisors who worked in children's day camps last summer. What a shame that not more of them come to benefit from it! Besides, I'm building some interesting relationships there."

"Is this letter an invitation to the next weekend?"

"No. This is a letter from the director, Béatrice Marceau. She's asking me to stop by the Francas' office, downtown, Saturday afternoon, to visit with them." She shrugged. "I don't know what they want, but I might just go—they are such good people!"

"Who are they?"

"Well, there's Béatrice, her brother Bertrand—who is married to an Algerian lady—and Jo Jeunet. They love children and it seems to me that all the children love them."

* * *

The Latin class was together again. The teacher scratched her throat. "I'm going to give you back the translations."

A religious silence hung over the room.

"First of all, I must congratulate you."

All the faces brightened.

"You did an excellent job as copyists. Unfortunately, this is not what I was expecting from you!"

The smiles disappeared.

"Madame, we've been overwhelmed with homework," Gilles protested.

"Very well. I won't penalize you this time. But I'll have to give you another translation."

The whole class groaned, but nobody dared to add anything else.

Once outside, they gathered together again. "Latin!"

"I like English so much better!"

"Hey! If you were allowed to dream, what country would you like to travel to?"

"Les États-Unis!"

"Yes, the United States of America . . . I hope I can go there at least once in my lifetime."

"Or Canada!"

"And you, Amanda, don't you have anything to say?"

Amanda was deeply immersed in a book by Frison Roche, La Piste Oubliée[5] "Sorry? What did you say?"

"Wouldn't you like to go to the United States?"

"What for? What's over there that we don't have?"

"Wouldn't you like to travel?"

"Sure I would, but not to the United States. This is so . . . common . . . "

The young people laughed. "Tell us where then!"

"Come on, today you're allowed to dream, and it doesn't cost anything."

---

[5]*The Forgotten Path.*

"You guess!"

"La Chine."

"Non."

"L'Inde."

"Maybe la Russie?"

"Le Japon?"

The young lady kept shaking her head. "Neither!"

"You tell us!"

"Do you give up?"

"We do!"

"Well . . . I'd like to see the Sahara."

"The Sahara?" Her classmates stared at her perplexedly. "Unbelievable!"

"But . . . there's nothing in the Sahara!"

"Just imagine Amanda in the middle of the Sahara, sitting by herself under an umbrella!" The picture was so funny they all burst out laughing.

"You're wrong," she answered gravely. "There are a lot of things in the desert. But one must see them with the heart."

"What, for instance?"

"Sky and land, as far as the eye can see—oasis, palm trees and . . . human beings."

"Gosh, that was close. You nearly convinced me!"

CAMARADES

ON SATURDAY AFTERNOON, AMANDA PUSHED on the door to the Francas' office. Bertrand and Béatrice were both sitting behind a table; Jo was perched on the top of another one. "Hi, sweetheart!" she greeted her.

Amanda went around to kiss them. "How are you all doing?"

"We're doing fine."

"Why did you ask me to come?"

"We just wanted to see your pretty face."

"All right, here it is."

"How do you like the training?"

"It's great, and I believe it's important. I get a lot of ideas, and there's a good atmosphere."

"That's exactly what we think!"

"Have you ever considered getting some real training—to obtain the national BAFA[6]?" Béatrice asked.

"You'd be better paid. You'd have a standard salary."

"Yes, of course, but . . ." Amanda was hesitant.

"But what?" Jo questioned sharply.

---

[6]BAFA: Brevet d'Aptitude aux Fonctions d'Animateurs. (National French certificate to work as a children's supervisor).

"I don't have the means to pay for the training, that's all."

"Hey, you worked last summer!"

"I did, but my full paycheck is going to defray the cost of the Conservatoire and other music expenses."

The three looked at each other. Bertrand turned to his sister. "This grant we have is a real problem. I really don't know who could benefit from it."

"That's right; it isn't easy to find serious people."

"Yeah!" Jo approved. "Actually, as I was saying, I can only think of one person!"

Amanda was starting to feel ill at ease. She turned her back on them and gazed through the window.

"Tell us, Amanda!" Bertrand called. "What do you think of the Francas?"

She shrugged. "What do I think of the Francas? Who cares! All I know is that you're good people."

"Well then, why don't you purchase a card from the party? Honestly, it's a bargain! If you can't afford dix francs[7], you're really bad off!" Jo declared.

"All we need is your signature, and we have a brand new card ready for you," encouraged Béatrice as she was waving a square of paper.

Amanda slowly turned around. She was unsettled. "No, I can't!"

There was a silence.

"Is it a money problem?"

"No, it isn't."

"What is it, then?" Bertrand asked gently.

---

[7]Equivalent to five dollars.

The situation had taken Amanda by surprise, and the three leaders of the Francas Association for La Serpe and its district were waiting for an answer. She sighed. "All right. I'm going to try to explain to you; I hope you'll understand."

She leaned against a third table and thought for a second. She remembered the little man who had come to visit the handful of Christians of La Serpe. She had bought a book from him, Pardonne-moi Natacha.[8]

"You see, the Francs Camarades is a communist movement, and I know from reliable sources that communists are by definition and in general atheists."

The three Francas nodded affirmatively.

"This in itself wouldn't bother me too much if they hadn't imposed their belief by force in some countries—among them, the U.S.S.R."

"The U.S.S.R. is far from here. Our own movement is typically French."

"I know, but it happens that Christianity is not only French but universal. Moreover, I consider myself to be a . . . Christian, and I know that I have brothers and sisters in the faith that have suffered tremendously in those countries—even in concentration camps—or who've been tortured. Out of solidarity with them, you'll understand that I wouldn't have a clear conscience if I gave even one penny to the party."

A heavy silence hovered in the room. Now, Amanda was waiting. Her friends looked at each other. Bertrand sighed. Finally, Béatrice spoke. "Listen, Amanda. We have a Francas grant that covers the training of one person for the BAFA. It covers the entire expense."

---

[8]*Forgive me, Natacha,* by Sergei Kourdakov

"It does. And honestly, we haven't found anyone else but you for that training," Jo went on.

"The question is: does she have to be a member of the party to benefit from the grant?" Bertrand asked the women.

"Don't worry about it," Amanda answered. "You'll find someone else."

"Allow us to do some research on it. We would really like this grant to go to you, if you care at all."

Amanda got the impression that everything was going too fast. "Well, I do. If it were possible, there would be no reason for me to refuse. I have nothing personal against you, and I rather appreciate you!"

"All right! You can count on us! As soon as we're better informed about this, we'll let you know."

"In any case, thanks to you all. Now, I've got to go!"

* * *

A week later, Amanda laid her bicycle against the wall of the day-camp center. As soon as she saw her, Jo ran to her. "Come quick! We have some news for you."

She led her to Béatrice and Bertrand's office.

"The grant is yours!" Béatrice declared. "However, there's one condition: You must commit to do your internship with us."

"Preferably with me!" Bertrand said. "I'll lead the camp in July."

"I'll lead it in August!" Béatrice added.

"Wonderful! I'll take the job. You know what—with you two as bosses, I think I'm going to work both months."

"I guess you just don't know what you're getting into."

"I think I do, and I like it!"

"The training will take place during the spring vacation in the vicinity of Montargis." Jo told her, handing her a paper with the information. "I'll be there too. I'll be a teacher, and there will be another trainee from La Serpe."

SPRING TRAINING

SPRING BREAK HAD ARRIVED WITH its mild weather and gorgeous fruit-trees gloriously blooming above the walls of La Serpe's private gardens. In the vicinity of Montargis, the BAFA training took place in a public boarding school. On the evening of the first day, a young man shyly stepped into the class.

"Welcome, Philippe!" the teacher said. "Let me introduce you. Philippe is from La Serpe. If I understand properly, he hasn't been able to join us earlier because he was working. Is that correct?"

"Yes, it is."

"Well, just find a place. We're just beginning a puppet workshop."

"Salut!" Amanda said, pausing from her attempt to get a wooden spoon all dressed up. "I'm from La Serpe too."

"Good evening," he answered politely.

"Except for Jo, we're the only ones from there. Do you know her?"

"Yes, we know each other."

The young man was kind. Soon he and Amanda started to select their workshops depending on the choice of the other, in order to be together as much as possible.

* * *

The ten days of training passed quickly. As they were nearing the end, Amanda and Philippe found each other in the courtyard during a break. The young man pulled a cigarette out of a pack. "Excuse me, but I smoke. I know it's a bad habit, but I haven't managed to stop yet. Actually, I haven't smoked so much here. They kept us busy."

"How old are you?"

"I'm nineteen. And you?"

"I've just turned seventeen."

He looked around. Nobody was near them. He hesitated and then said, "Listen, I'd like to ask you something."

"Sure. What is it?"

"Would you like to go out with me?"

Amanda's eyes opened with surprise. "Go out? But we're already out." With both hands, she showed the open sky. "What else would you like?"

He observed her for a few seconds. She was awfully serious. "All right. Just . . . drop it!"

"Well, what did you mean?"

He smiled gently. "Nothing, I'm telling you. Just don't worry about it."

The last class was starting. They went in.

The teacher addressed the class. "Tonight, we're going to learn a country dance specifically for teenagers. To start, we have to stand two by two, if possible a boy and a girl."

Philippe and Amanda got together right away. The teacher chose Jo to demonstrate. She started up the music. "Watch these first steps. They're easy. Next, the guy makes the girl twirl. Now, watch carefully! The 'cavalier' bends one knee to the ground and holding her hand, he guides his partner as she walks around him. That's all. You see it's not very complicated."

Amanda thought she was not the most gracious dancer, but her partner was charming. However, the last evening was over quickly. Before going up to their rooms, Amanda and Philippe stopped in the hall.

"How are you getting home tomorrow?" she asked.

"The same way I came!"

"How's that?"

"Hitchhiking! And you?"

"I'm taking the bus. The Trans-Beauce. Why don't you take it?"

"Hitchhiking is much cheaper."

"I thought you had a job."

"I do, in a factory."

"You must have enough money then?"

"I'm the family breadwinner. My mother is a widow, and I'm the oldest of five children."

"My! When I think of it, you have a point. I don't have any money either. My parents are covering the expense for my trip."

"If you'd like to, you can come with me."

"I'd love to—but I don't want to be a hindrance."

"On the contrary! Hitchhiking is much easier with a girl. It helps people trust."

"It's okay, then. Remember, you were talking about going out together? I've got to tell my parents though. I'll call my neighbors, since we don't have a telephone at home."

* * *

The next day, after breakfast, the two young people said goodbye to their classmates.

"I'm sorry," Jo excused herself. "My car is packed full of stuff, and I can't take any of you. Should I arrive before you, I'll come back to meet you."

They loaded their backpacks and started for the entry to the village.

"This is probably going to be our longest wait because it's the most remote," Philippe explained.

"You're experienced, aren't you? It's okay with me. The sun is starting to warm things up."

Philippe was keeping an eye on his watch. "It's been ten minutes already."

A car stopped. "I can take you to a turn-off twenty kilometers from here."

"It's better than nothing."

"Get in!"

When the driver stopped, he left them off in the middle of some fields. The sprouting barley looked like grass. A lark was singing high in the sky.

"Man! I'm sorry," Philippe apologized. "This place is worse than the first one."

"I find it beautiful," she retorted.

He smiled. "Maybe, but not for hitchhiking!"

"Should we walk?"

"No. We wouldn't get very far. At least here we're at a crossroads—and I feel kind of responsible to get you home."

"I told you I would hinder you!"

"It has nothing to do with that. I'm glad I'm not alone. It's less boring."

Half an hour later, a truck stopped.

"Good morning!"

"I'm going to Chartres."

"It's perfect!"

"Climb in!"

"I don't remember ever riding in such a big truck," Amanda said with her most beautiful smile. The man didn't reply. Philippe didn't try conversing, so she decided to keep quiet. The warmth of the cabin and the hum of the engine began to rock her to sleep.

* * *

A few hours later, a car dropped the young people off at another crossroads.

"Twenty more kilometers and we'll be at La Serpe," Philippe remarked, relieved.

"Not bad! It's not four o'clock yet."

Suddenly, a car passed by them, beeping furiously—then stopped with a strident squealing of brakes.

"It's Jo!" Amanda screamed.

Jo was laughing. "Come on, get in. I was afraid I might miss you. Considering your speed though, I'd have had plenty of time to make the trip twice back and forth."

"You exaggerate!"

As an answer, Jo started to sing loudly. "La tut-tut pouêt-pouêt la voilà, la totomobile, la tut-tut pouêt-pouêt la voilà! Qu'est-ce qu'elle fait donc là?"[9]

[9]Children's French song: Beep beep, honk honk, here it comes, the little car . . . Beep beep, honk honk, here it comes! What is it doing here?

A BOYFRIEND

A WEEK HAD PASSED SINCE the last school term had started. At four p.m., at the entrance to the school grounds, students were gathering into small groups; cars were starting. Claire and Amanda were cutting their way through the crowd.

"Amanda!"

Amanda looked around. A young blond man, sitting on a motorcycle, waved to her. He was smiling. Without thinking, she headed toward him right away.

"See you tomorrow," Claire shouted, moving away rapidly.

"Philippe! What are you doing here?"

"If you'd like, I'll take you back home tonight."

"With this?" She pointed to the vehicle.

"Yes."

"You know, the road climbs sharply to go to my home."

"We won't get any speeding ticket, that's for sure, but the machine is strong."

Philippe gave the pedal a push to start the engine.

"Do you know I've never ridden on a motorcycle?"

"It's your chance to try."

"Please, don't make fun of me."

"Just come. Don't be afraid."

The saddle was long and made for two people. Amanda took her place behind the rider. She grabbed hold of his black coat. "Why didn't you come last week?"

"I'm working rotating shifts. Last week, I worked in the evenings. Tell me, would it bother you if I come again to get you tomorrow?"

"Tomorrow, I'll leave the school at four."

* * *

At the end of the week, for the fourth time, Amanda got off the motorcycle. Philippe had just stopped on the parking spot in front of her home. The spring sun was still high in the sky, and the entry door to the house was wide open to let in the warmth of the day.

Amanda smiled. "Oh, I just remembered that it's Friday, and Maman comes home early. She's here. I'd like to introduce you to her. I've talked to her about you. Would you come in?"

"Well . . . All right!"

Louise stuck her head out the door as Philippe walked slowly up the path.

"Good evening, madame."

"Good evening, young man. It's really kind of you to bring my daughter back home."

"It's my pleasure."

Louise started a little conversation. "Would you like to come in?" she offered.

"No, thank you. I must go back home."

"Au revoir, alors."

"Au revoir, madame."

Amanda accompanied Philippe to the motorcycle. He wasn't in a hurry anymore.

"Tomorrow is Saturday."

"Yes. So?"

"I won't go to get you at the school . . . Maybe we could still see each other, go out somewhere in the afternoon or in the evening. What do you think?"

"I don't know. Where would you like to go?"

"I have no idea. Maybe . . . to a café."

"I hate cafés. They stink of alcohol and cigarette smoke, and they're noisy. I'd feel so ill at ease there!"

"As you wish!"

"Well, where then?"

"I don't know. Could I just come and visit with you here tomorrow?"

"Sure, if you'd like. I'll wait for you around four."

"D'accord!"

He started his motorcycle. "Au revoir!"

"See you tomorrow!"

* * *

Amanda went back to the house. "Maman, you were wonderful with him."

Louise smiled. "He's a handsome lad, and also very kind and serious."

"Really? You like him?"

"I'd say yes."

"Tomorrow is Saturday, and he asked me if I wanted to go out with him."

"What did you say, then?"

Amanda sat on the couch. "He wanted to go to a café. I told him I didn't like that kind of a place, so he'll simply come here."

"Is he your type of guy?"

"Why are you asking me that question?"

"You see, Amanda, I have the impression that this young man is starting to get seriously attached to you. If he is what you want, that's okay, but if he is not your type, the sooner he knows it, the better."

"I hadn't thought of that. It hasn't even been a month since we met each other, and he's been a very good friend to me."

"I think that at this juncture you can't think only about yourself. You have to consider him and his feelings also."

"You're right, Maman. Actually, he's not at all what I'd like in a man. I know what I want by heart. At the top of the list, I want a Christian. Next to that, I want a man who doesn't smoke and doesn't go to the cafés. He's already broken all these criteria. Tomorrow, I'll talk to him."

Her mother sighed. "For goodness sake, Amanda, go easy on him."

"Don't worry. I'll manage."

* * *

The next day, Philippe was on time. Amanda went out to meet him. He stopped the engine of his vehicle. "Hi!"

"Salut."

"Are we going on a walk?"

"Philippe, I've got to talk to you."

"Sure, what is it?"

"I think it would be best if we don't go out together anymore."

"May I know why?"

Amanda perceived hurt in his voice. "Of course. The problem is . . . I don't want to go out with someone I'm not going to marry. The day I'll go out with a man, it'll be with the intention of getting married."

The blue eyes were making a visible effort to understand. "I'm not against marriage."

It became difficult for Amanda to sustain his stare. She blinked. "I'm still too young for this."

"There's no hurry."

"Certainly, but that's not all."

Philippe braced himself and stopped breathing.

"The man I'll marry will have to be a Christian, a born-again Christian. Do you understand this?"

By now, he was pale. "Yes, I do," he answered softly. He got onto his two wheels. The engine roared. "Farewell," he said without looking at her.

"Adieu."

The motorcycle disappeared at the turn of the road. Amanda stood on the parking spot for a while, listening to the sound of the engine slowly dying behind the dwellings, hoping it would not go off.

EXAMINATIONS

AMANDA WAS SLOWLY COMING BACK home from school. Every day she walked up a narrow road bordered by an old stone wall, a vestige of the rampart of an ancient castle. On the other side of the wall, purple, red, and white lilacs were in full bloom, overflowing on the top of the whole length of the fortifications. She deeply breathed in their sweet fragrance. The road continued on along the crest of a hillside. About half way, she stopped. On her right-hand side was a full opening on a beautiful landscape. The blue of the sky was so transparent it almost seemed unreal. The entire town spread at her feet.

"Lord!" she prayed. "So many souls in this city don't know their right hand from their left; and there are so many Muslims here." Something in the atmosphere seemed sacred. She added, "I'll be a missionary in North Africa."

She shivered and then started back on her way. At the end of the road, her path joined the main street. Her mother was there, just arriving from work; they met at the crossroad. Amanda smiled. "Maman, I'm so glad to see you. I've got some great news for you. Someday, I'll be a missionary in North Africa."

Louise lost her composure. "My poor girl. Are you losing your mind?"

The smile disappeared. "Don't worry, Maman. It's not going to happen soon."

When the two women arrived at home, they were silent.

* * *

Mid-June at the Conservatoire de Versailles, Amanda took her first official viola exam. When she came out of the examination room, viola in hand, she was white and shaking all over. She leaned against the wall.

"Are you okay?" Véronique asked.

"I was shaking so much that it's been a catastrophe."

"Please, wait here for me!" her friend pleaded.

M. Villemin emerged from the room and asked Véronique to enter. When she came out, she was as pale and shaky as her friend. There was only one student left.

"At this point, let's wait for the results," Véronique murmured.

Finally, M. Villemin came out for good. He shook his head and disappeared at the corner of the stairs, without a word. The secretary pinned the results up on the board. Both girls had obtained only a third medal—had flunked!

Véronique greeted her friend and quickly left the place. Amanda slowly went down to the courtyard and passed by the viola room. The bare bulb was crudely shining in the back. M. Villemin was playing. She listened and, attracted by the music, entered the room. The violist saw her and stopped. He put his instrument away. "Amanda!" he said suddenly. "I'm disappointed."

She didn't answer. He turned to her and stared deeply into the desolate eyes. "Notice, I'm not disappointed in you; no, not at all. I'm disappointed because I know what you are able to do. However, I didn't know you were capable of shaking so much. I promise you I have means to make it pass."

Amanda's face brightened. "Really?"

"Yes, besides, you haven't wasted your efforts. You've learned a new clef, a new instrument, and you've been improving a lot."

"Merci, monsieur!"

"I hope you're ready to start again in September. You see, with the viola, it's not like with the violin. You still have two years left to advance to the required level." He had his little mischievous smile.

"I'll be here in September. Have a good summer, Monsieur Villemin."

"You too. Just what are you going to do this summer?"

"I'm going to work in day camps all summer. That will pay for the lessons here."

"Take care then. Good-bye!"

* * *

On the platform of the station in Versailles, Amanda recognized Cédric. They briefly greeted each other and got onto the train. They found a place where they could sit face to face. "So, how is it going with you?" Cédric asked, once the train was rolling.

"I just failed my first viola exam, but I still have two years left to make it. What about you?"

"I flunked the violin exam to enter the Conservatoire de Paris. But I intend to try one more time in September."

"Do you have any hope of making it?"

"Nope!"

"If you don't, who will?"

"What do you mean?"

"You are gifted . . . and you work hard."

"You just don't know how it works. Paris has the only professional music school in France, and they already know in advance who's going to get in. To reach that level without having pull is impossible."

"Why are you going to try again, then?"

He shrugged. He didn't try to hide the truth: he was discouraged.

"I heard they're going to open a second Conservatoire National in Lyon," Amanda remarked.

"That's true, but it's not going to make any difference. The system will be the same."

"I heard that Monsieur Villemin is to be nominated for there. Besides, in Versailles, good viola players are rare. He could give you some pull."

"Mind you, I've already thought about that!"

The two young people were quiet for a while. Amanda started again. "You'd miss the chanterelle,[10] wouldn't you?"

He stared at her strangely.

"But you'd win another string, the C one. It sounds like velvet!" she encouraged.

He nodded. "In September, I'll try again to enter Paris. Then, I'll go to register with Monsieur Villemin."

* * *

[10]The chanterelle is the E-string, the highest one on a violin, and very much used by soloists.

Toward the end of June, Amanda passed her Baccalauréat de Français[11] without any problem.

[11]Le Bac Français: Important national examination in French taken at the end of eleventh grade.

THE END OF A ROMANCE

A FEW DAYS LATER, BERTRAND Marceau assembled all the July camp supervisors. "Amanda, what age group would you like to oversee?"

"I'd like to start with the little ones."

"You'll be with Céline, then."

"Great!"

"Jo?"

"I want the teenagers."

"Philippe?"

"Same."

"You two will be together. Christiane and Alain, are you okay with the juniors? "

"No problem."

Bertrand went down his list. He had employed twelve supervisors. "I want your days to be well prepared and organized. Get to work right now for tomorrow."

Amanda glanced at Philippe. He hadn't greeted or even acknowledged her. He was keeping as far away from her as possible. She realized he was still hurt and felt the best she could do was to respect his distance.

* * *

The July day camp functioned at its full capacity. There was a scheduled coffee break for half of the supervisors at one o'clock. "Amanda, would you care for some coffee?"

"No thanks, I don't drink coffee yet. I prefer Kool-aid, like my little ones."

Bertrand started to compliment the group. "We've had a good month. I'm happy with you all. The activities have been going great, and we're already in our final week. To reward you, I propose that you enjoy an evening among yourselves. I'll leave you the whole center—the kitchen too—and you can do as you wish. I promise I won't come to bother you."

"You mean, just the supervisors?"

"Hé! Bonne idée."

"Who wouldn't come?"

"How about we do this tomorrow night?"

The team started to discuss plans for a meal.

"It's already one thirty," Bertrand interrupted soon. "Back to work! Think of your colleagues!"

"I'm going to relieve Céline," Amanda said.

As she was going out, Céline saw her and came to meet her. "Un petit café!"[12] she said.

"Un petit qu'a fait?"[13] Amanda answered, playing on the words.

They looked at each other and burst out laughing.

"Céline, tomorrow evening we're having a party."

"I can't come. I have a rendezvous with my boyfriend."

---

[12]A little coffee!

[13]A little one messed up his pants?

"Too bad."

"Hurry up! The kids are all by themselves."

"I'm going!"

* * *

The next evening, everyone had gone to great lengths to make a good meal. While Amanda prepared vinaigrette for her salad, Jo sang softly as she watched her pot of curried rice slowly cook on the stove.

"Qui peut faire de la voile sans vent ? Qui peut ramer sans rame? Et qui peut quitter son ami, sans verser de larmes."[14]

The boys were outside talking. "It's ready. Come to the table!" Christiane called.

Philippe sat on the side opposite to where Amanda was. He was quiet and hardly touched his food. He only drank the wine that had been served.

* * *

As the meal drew to a close, the young people began to sing summer songs. Philippe didn't open his mouth.

"Come on, Philippe, don't make such a face!" Jo sighed.

"He's nothing like he used to be anymore," Christiane remarked.

The others couldn't help glancing at Amanda, who acted as if she hadn't heard anything. Philippe poured himself a second glass of wine and drank it slowly.

"Let's play some games," someone suggested.

"Dishes first!" Jo ordered. "Who wants to wash the dishes?"

Christiane turned to Amanda. "Try to go talk to him."

---

[14]Who can sail without wind? Who can row without an oar? And who can leave his (or her) friend without a tear?

Amanda got up right away. "I'll wash the dishes."

The boys helped with cleaning the table. Philippe didn't move. He poured himself a third glassful of wine. Jo grabbed the bottle. "Easy on the wine!"

Philippe got up, left the full glass on the table, and went outside without a word.

"Bon sang!" Alain exclaimed. "Our friend is not doing well."

"Ouais! And he's been like this for a while!" Jo remarked.

"He wasn't like this before."

"He is miserable."

Christiane went outside. When she came back in, Amanda was already washing the pots and pans. "Amanda! For goodness sake, do something!"

"I'm already washing dishes. Can't you see?"

"I'll finish up for you."

"Why? Do you mean I'm too slow?"

"Amanda, don't play stupid. Philippe is suffering and it's your fault!"

"Might be true!" Jo added, while she wiped the dishes.

Amanda held her hands up in the air, full of soapy foam. She half turned around. "What do you want me to do?"

"Go talk to him!"

"Go comfort him!" Alain threw in.

"No!" she answered softly. "It's impossible."

"Don't you have a heart?" Christiane shouted angrily.

"If it upsets you so much, why don't you try to comfort him?" Amanda replied.

The disturbed girl tried to calm down. "I just gave it a try. He . . . He is crying. I couldn't do anything. It's up to you!"

"No . . . All I could do . . . It wouldn't do any good!" Amanda was now facing the whole team. "Try to understand. There's nothing I can do. It all hangs on you now."

The supervisors looked at each other. Alain sighed. "You're right. You've done enough harm. I'm going to take Philippe home."

He put his vest on and went out into the dark. Amanda was leaning against the sink. She wasn't moving; the foam on her hands was slowly vanishing.

"Come on," Jo said. "Get out of here. I'll wash and you dry, and then I'll take you home."

Amanda obeyed without thinking, taking the towel from Jo's hands. The evening ended up abruptly.

* * *

That night, Jo was driving slowly. She broke the silence: "You believe in God, don't you?"

"Yes, I do."

"I used to believe in God when I was little."

"And now?"

"It's been a long time since I stopped believing."

"Why so?"

"When I consider all the evil that's going on in the world, I just can't believe in God."

"You mean you believe there's a God, but you don't believe He's good?"

"Oh no! I don't believe that God exists at all. If He exists and if He is almighty—as believers say—why does he allow all that is evil to happen?"

Amanda was frowning. "All right; well, if He doesn't exist, at least you can't accuse Him of all the evils."

"That's right. Where does evil come from then?"

"I don't know," Amanda admitted humbly. "But I do believe God exists and He's good. Therefore, evil comes from someone else who's bad."

Jo sighed. "We've arrived!" She stopped her car on the parking lot.

Amanda was thinking. "You know, Jo, God Himself suffered the consequences of the evil in our world. He was crucified. However, the good news is that He rose from the dead. He's alive."

"Well, I'm afraid this is too complicated for my little brain."

"I don't think so. It's worth being reconciled with Him." Amanda opened the door of the car. "Thanks for the drive, Jo! Bye!"

SCOUT MEETING

IN SEPTEMBER 1979, AMANDA ENTERED in Terminal[15], still in the literary track.

Two months went by until one day, the social studies teacher, M. Gréfort, handed the class two historical texts, written by Voltaire and Rousseau, denying the existence of God. He was a gentle little man with white hair and gold-framed glasses. He gave his students a few minutes to read the texts, and then he called back their attention. "Does anyone here believe in God?"

Amanda boldly raised her hand. As she was the only one, the teacher suddenly decided to give her the honor of a speech. "Would you please stand up and explain to us how you've come to believe in God?"

"I believe in God because, one day, He revealed Himself to me."

"Well, I'd love to believe in God," the puzzled teacher said, "but I just can't. How could I believe?"

"You can start by reading the Bible. If God exists, then He is true to His Word, and here is what He says: 'He who seeks shall find and to the one who knocks, it will be opened.' If you truly seek Him with all your heart, He'll find you."

[15]Twelfth grade.

Just then, the bell rang, leaving the bearded teacher shaking his head.

In the schoolyard, Gilles, Denise, and a few others from her class surrounded Amanda. "We've understood you have faith in God."

"It's true."

"We are scouts from Saint-André's Catholic Church of La Serpe."

"All right! It's a big church," she remarked.

"Once a month, we meet together for a discovery evening."

"We would like to invite you. Would you come?"

"What do you do there?"

"Usually we study a Bible text."

"We share what we believe."

"We can ask questions and seek answers."

"Father Raphaël is the leader. He's amazing. You'll see."

Amanda smiled. "I'd love to come. When is the next meeting?"

"This coming Friday at seven p.m., at Saint-André's Church."

"I'll be there."

* * *

At Saint-André's Church, the meeting room was austere. A dozen young people Amanda's age had gathered together around tables set in the shape of a horseshoe. Father Raphaël was a man full of energy, influential with the youth. After a long introduction, he said, "Let's read the text of the Gospel of Saint-Jean, chapter one, verses 44 to 51."[16]

One of the youth started to read. "Now Philip was from Bethsaida, of the city of Andrew and Peter. Philip found Nathanael and said to him, 'We have found Him of whom Moses in the Law and also the

---

[16]All Scriptures mentioned here are from the New American Standard Bible published by Zondervan.

Prophets wrote—Jesus of Nazareth, the son of Joseph.' Nathanael said to him, 'Can any good thing come out of Nazareth?' Philip said to him, 'Come and see.' Jesus saw Nathanael coming to Him, and he said of him, 'Behold, an Israelite indeed, in whom there is no deceit!' Nathanael said to Him, 'How do you know me?' Jesus answered and said to him, 'Before Philip called you, when you were under the fig tree, I saw you.' Nathanael answered Him, 'Rabbi, You are the Son of God; You are the king of Israel.' Jesus answered and said to him, 'Because I said to you that I saw you under the fig tree, do you believe? You will see greater things than these.' And He said to him, 'Truly, truly, I say to you, you will see the heavens opened and the angels of God ascending and descending on the Son of Man.'"

"What did you understand from this text?" the priest asked. "Do you have any questions?"

Gilles began. "Father Raphaël, I admit I don't believe. It's too difficult for me. I feel like I'm in a dark tunnel. However, I'd love to have faith, to see the end of the tunnel. What should I do?"

Father Raphaël thought rapidly. "Don't worry about that. If this could help you, I'm going to confess something. When I was ordained as a priest, I didn't believe in God either. I was an atheist. I too felt like I was in a tunnel. But don't be discouraged. One day or another we come to the end of the tunnel and we see light. You are still young. The important thing is to not stop on the way but to keep searching."

"How long has it been since you've believed in God?"

"Only a few years."

Amanda raised her hand. "I'd like to say something to my friend also. If you can't see daylight, God knows exactly where you are. He knows your heart is searching for Him. In the text we just read, it's clear God had seen Nathanael and He knew him before Nathanael ever discovered Him. Jesus was waiting to meet Nathanael to reveal Himself to him. I find these words encouraging for one who seeks."

When the meeting ended, Amanda's friends came to her. "Did you like it?"

"Sure! I'll come back."

IMMUNIZATIONS

ON MONDAY MORNING, AMANDA'S TWELFTH-GRADE class was working through an English lesson when someone knocked at the door.

"Come in!"

A nurse entered. She delivered a stack of papers to the teacher: "This is for distribution," she said. "By the way, I'm looking for Amanda Vissac!"

Amanda raised her hand. "It's me, madame!"

"For nearly three years you've been enrolled in this school, and I still don't have your immunization records! How come? I've never seen this happen before!"

"I'm sorry, madame. I'll tell my parents about it."

"You are required to bring it to me as soon as possible. I need it. There's going to be a tuberculin test in the class next week."

"I'm very sorry, madame!"

"Besides," the nurse threatened, "you won't be able to take your baccalauréat exams without proper immunization records!" She left in a very bad temper.

* * *

At home that evening, Amanda related the incident of the day to her parents. She read aloud the paper that the nurse had given out. "B.C.G. Mandatory Immunization. All twelfth-grade students whose tuberculin test was administered over a year ago—whether positive or negative, or done any way other than the intra-dermal reaction or the Mono test—must participate. Both the control and re-immunization will be done at the school: the control, in the classrooms on Tuesday, November 20, 1979, in the morning; the reading of the control, in the classrooms on Friday, November 23, 1979, in the morning. Re-immunization will be done at the infirmary on Friday, November 23, 1979."[17]

Louise sighed. "When you were younger, I was always able to talk to understanding school directors. But in a large school like this, it's nearly impossible to have a meaningful discussion anymore."

"Especially with medical professionals," Amanda agreed. "What shall I do then? If I had to explain to them why I'm not immunized, I don't think I'd be able to."

Armand suddenly looked up. "Actually, it's time you understand why we don't want you to be immunized. Meanwhile, it's simple: you won't be attending school Tuesday morning or Friday all day. I take full responsibility for it. If someone needs an explanation, it's my duty to give it. If they should ask you any questions, simply tell them we don't want you to be immunized; if this is not enough, tell them I'm ready to come to talk to them."

---

[17]In France, at this time, some laws were enforced in public health matters. Up to five different immunizations were mandatory throughout the country. With the passing of time, the French are looking for more enticing measures. Only three immunizations are still mandatory; however, the penalties are heavier.

Amanda nodded. Armand Vissac got up and went to the tallboy standing in the entryway. A mirror covered most of its surface. He pulled out a large bottom drawer and rummaged through it. He extracted a file and handed it to his daughter. "Here, read this. It'll give you some insight into the matter."

Amanda took the file and slipped into her room. There she spent several hours immersed in the documentation. As she neared the end of the folder, a paragraph caught her attention. She read it again thoughtfully: "Penalties incurred for refusal of inoculations are as follows: Smallpox, diphtheria, tetanus: F 600 to 1000, plus ten days to one month in prison; Poliomyelitis: Idem, and in case of a second offense, F 2000 and two months in prison; B.C.G.: F 40."

She stared in front of her and began to count on her fingers: "December, January, February, March, April."

She gathered up the documents and placed them on the living room table where her father was reading. "Here, Papa. I've read it all."

"Well then, what have you concluded?"

"I understand immunizations are in fact the fruit of a theory, and its consequences have never been fully checked scientifically."

"However," her father argued, "it is maintained that immunizations have caused the occurrence of epidemics to greatly diminish."

Amanda started to walk back and forth in the living room. "That's true. But it seems this argument has some weaknesses. In fact, epidemics have disappeared in a similar way in countries where immunizations were not practiced as well as in countries where they were practiced. Moreover, some diseases have totally disappeared from the surface of the earth even without the aid of immunizations. For instance, the bubonic plague—which claimed the life of King

Saint-Louis as he was coming back from a crusade." She suddenly stopped. "But then, how do we explain the lessening of epidemics?"

"This is a good question. Actually, epidemics started to vanish at the same time as hygiene and better nutrition became generalized due to technical progress. Unfortunately, improved hygiene and immunizations occurred at the same time."

"On the other hand," Amanda continued, "it seems that immunizations don't merely offer advantages, they also have their inconveniences—sometimes in the form of injuries to health. These have usually been kept secret, at least to the general public."

"That's right. Some medical doctors are fully aware of that, but they don't have the ability to rise up against the established medical order lest they suffer by having their licenses to legally exercise their medical skills removed."

"If immunizations present advantages for some and inconveniences for others, why doesn't the government simply let people choose?"

"This is another battlefront. This one is not solely on the medical level anymore, but on the ethical level. Pope Pius XII declared, 'The public authority holds without a doubt a direct authority and has the right to impose demands on the activities of parties, but in no case can it dispose directly of its physical being . . . This is an abuse of the competence of an authority.'"

"In other words," Amanda said thoughtfully, "even if the medical profession and the state are both fully correct, they have no right to force us into anything as far as our own bodies are concerned. I dare say that if I can choose between falling sick under the hand of God or under the hand of men, I'd rather choose the hand of God."

"Without a doubt. However, I want to be perfectly clear with you. I don't contend only for freedom of conscience and choice. I also believe that immunizations are basically harmful."

"If the deal is so bad, why do we immunize at all?"

"Here is what constitutes the bottom of the problem. Do you know what country has the most mandatory immunizations in the world?"

"France, I suppose."

"And do you know where the biggest pharmaceutical companies are found?"

"In France also."

"Well then, you understand!"

"You mean . . ."

"I mean that huge financial interests are involved. They use and abuse the weaknesses and fears of the great majority. The media, by the way, does a great job in keeping them all alive and prospering."

"Papa, do you know that you are liable to a fine—and even prison—because you never had me immunized?"

Armand Vissac shrugged. "I'm not worried about that!"

"In only five months, I'll reach majority, and therefore I'll be responsible for my own choices. At least, you'll be out of danger."

"Well, then, I hope you're not worrying for me!"

"I think I am. In any case, I'll try to make as few waves as possible."

Amanda disappeared into her room while her father sat there, thoughtful. He shook his head.

THE CHALLENGE

AT THE BEGINNING OF THE month of January, the scouts of the community of Saint-André Church gathered again around Father Raphaël. "Today, we'll read in the Gospel of Saint-Matthew, chapter 12, verses 38 to 41."

A young lady undertook the reading. "Then some of the scribes and Pharisees said to Him, 'Teacher, we want to see a sign from You.' But He answered and said to them, 'An evil and adulterous generation craves for a sign; and yet no sign will be given to it but the sign of Jonah the prophet; for just as Jonah was three days and three nights in the belly of the sea monster, so will the Son of Man be three days and three nights in the heart of the earth.

"The men of Nineveh will stand up with this generation at the judgment, and will condemn it because they repented at the preaching of Jonah; and behold, something greater than Jonah is here.'"

"What do you understand from this text?" Father Raphaël asked.

"This text gives us a picture."

"Yes, there is a picture here," Father Raphaël responded. "What is this picture about?"

The young people were thinking hard. Amanda spoke up. "Jesus announces His death and resurrection."

"Yes, He announces the cross. And how does He do that?"

"He tells a story," somebody else answered.

"What is the relation between the story and the cross?"

Again, there was silence while everyone kept thinking, but answers were not coming.

"The story might be a bit disconcerting," Father Raphaël admitted. "Yes, Amanda?"

"Jesus presents Himself as being greater than Jonah. He is talking about His divinity. Therefore, He could perform a sign, but He knows that the scribes and the Pharisees don't and won't believe in Him. The only miracle that will truly prove who He is, is His resurrection from the dead. Jesus doesn't let them manipulate Him. This is the only miracle they'll see."

"Good!"

"I don't understand what this tale of Jonah is about," one of the youth threw in.

Amanda raised her hand again. "When the prophet Jonah was swallowed by a great sea animal, the Bible says he stayed three days and three nights in its belly before being spit out alive. This in itself is a true miracle—in which all the Jews of that time believed. It was also given as a prophetic sign of the death and resurrection of Jesus."

Some of the teenagers looked perplexed. Hands were quickly rising up. "Did Jonah truly exist?"

"Isn't it rather a myth?"

"It's a legend, isn't it?"

"All right, all right," the priest stepped in. "I don't think Amanda really meant that Jonah is a historical character."

Amanda innocently answered. "But yes, I believe that Jonah truly existed!"

"He might have. But this story of the fish can't be real."

"If it was not amazing, it wouldn't be talked about as a miracle," Amanda asserted.

The young people reacted. Hands were rising up again. The priest said. "In our time, everybody knows it's a legend. You can't truly believe this, can you?"

"Monsieur," Amanda answered, perplexed at the priest's beliefs, "the Bible doesn't lie. If it tells us it's a true story, then it is."

The priest smiled. "Of course. The Bible tells a lot of other things and everyone knows very well, in our time, it's fiction. The Bible talks about angels too. Now, don't tell me you also believe in angels!"

Amanda opened her mouth. Everybody was silent, but eyes were smiling. They were all suspended, watching her lips. She slightly blushed but answered firmly. "The Bible tells us there were angels present at the birth of Jesus Christ. If we don't believe in the angels anymore, why should we still believe in Christ? Oui, monsieur! I believe in angels."

Father Raphaël couldn't help laughing. The young people were trying not to—out of deference for their guest friend.

"My goodness! I really thought nobody believed this anymore. You are truly naïve."

With raised eyebrows, Amanda asked, "Well then, what remains to be believed from the Bible?"

"Listen, young lady, we're going to stop our talk right here. However, I challenge you to find one single exegete who still believes in the story of Jonah!"

Amanda clenched her teeth. She wrote one word on the piece of white paper that was in front of her—EXEGETE—for she had never heard this word before.

After the priest had concluded the class, Amanda went up to Gilles and Denise.

"I'm sorry, but I don't think I'll be coming back again. I just wanted to let you know."

"What a shame!" they sighed disappointedly. "You were really bringing in some spirit."

"I might come back here one more time though," she added mysteriously.

* * *

Back home, Amanda got some writing paper out and started a letter. She wrote the address on the envelope: "Radio-Evangile, B.P. 30, 06240 Beausoleil." She posted it. About one week later, she received an answer.

* * *

The month of January, with its cool and damp weather, was coming to an end. Amanda prayed, put the precious letter in her coat pocket, and walked out of her house. She went down the hill, stopped downtown to make a copy, and started up the other side of the hill. The sky was blue and the sun was brightly shining, but it barely warmed up the atmosphere. However, Amanda's walk through the whole city warmed her up. She arrived at Saint-André's Catholic

Church with pink cheeks and entered the modern building where the meetings took place. It was empty. She climbed up a stair and then wandered down a long corridor on which several doors opened. A man came out of one of them. "Are you looking for someone?"

"Yes, please. Is Father Raphaël here?"

"Do you have an appointment?"

"Non, monsieur."

"Wait for me a minute. I'm going to see if I can find him."

"Thank you."

She waited several minutes that seemed endless. She drew a long breath and made sure the stairs to the exit were close enough. Finally, the man came back, accompanied by Father Raphaël.

"Good morning, Amanda. What do you want?"

"I came to talk to you."

"Well, I'll leave you, then," the other man said as he walked away.

The priest opened the door of the closest room. It was empty. "Do you want to go in?"

"No, thank you. I only want to give you this."

"What is it?"

"It's a letter."

She was ready to leave, but he opened the envelope in front of her. "Wait a minute," he said.

He pulled the paper out. She held her breath. He started to read aloud:

> *Dear young lady, Radio-Evangile has asked me to answer your letter of January 6th concerning Jonah. Because the priest you are referring to asked you to find an exegete who affirms the*

historicity of Jonah, I will put on my title. I'm not used to putting forward my degrees, but in this case I think it's good for you to know that I am not only a pastor but also a Doctor in Theology, have specialized in biblical Greek, and I have a license in Literature (Latin-Greek). I have taught exegesis for seventeen years in a Protestant Theological Faculty. Naturally, I am also skilled in Hebrew and exegesis of the Old Testament.

It is true that it is the fashion now in France and in some theological circles to deny the historicity of numerous biblical passages and biblical facts. The brain behind this way of thinking is a German theologian whose name is Bultmann. He propounds that the Bible is full of parables and myths. (Fiction, as your priest would say.)

Yes! There are a lot of parables; however, when it is question of parables, this is stated very clearly. It is dangerous to call "fiction" events that have been passed onto us as historical—and this can lead very far; for example, to the denial of the virgin birth, the bodily resurrection of Jesus, etc.

Jonah was a prophet (II Kings 14:25). The style of his book is that of a historical account. The names are not symbolic. Jesus used the story of Jonah without doubting its authenticity: three days and three nights in the belly of the great fish, like Jesus will stay in the tomb before His resurrection; Jesus recalls the historical event of the conversion of the Ninevites (Matthew 12:39 to 41; Luke 11:29 to 32). How can we contest the authority of Jesus? Are we going to object to the historicity of the "great fish" and of the miracle? We must then reject all miracles.

Archaeological discovery has brought to light the ruins of Nineveh, which did exist and which was as huge as the Bible describes it. The objections of style (Aramaisms) don't have any value. It is possible that the Ninevites converted (in part at least) because their empire was in a precarious state around 765 before Christ.

It is probably Jonah himself who wrote this book at his return from Nineveh.

Let us be firmly attached to what the Bible says, following the example of Jesus Christ with Jonah. May God bless your witness!

The priest slowly folded the letter. He finally looked at her. "So, you took it seriously, didn't you?"

"It was serious!"

"You shouldn't have!"

She stared at him, perplexed. "I also wanted to tell you that I won't be coming back."

"Do as you wish." He handed her the letter.

She stepped back. "No, you keep it! I don't need it, and it's for you. I have a copy. Bye!"

Quick as lightning, she turned around and disappeared down the stairs.

PHILOSOPHY

IN THE MIDDLE OF WINTER, as the philosophy class started, the teacher wrote a list of themes on the board. "There!" she said. "I'd like each one of you to do a presentation on one of the themes suggested here or on a theme of your choice. You can also work on it as a group of two."

Amanda raised her hand. "I'll take the theme on death."

"Could I do it with you?" Jocelyne asked her right away.

"I'd rather treat the subject alone."

"I've seen death very close," Jocelyne insisted. "I tried to commit suicide."

Amanda wavered. "Sorry, Jocelyne, but I do have my own ideas on the subject!"

"It's all right!" her classmate sighed, disappointed.

* * *

Later that day, after M. Gréfort finished a lecture on Japan, the students departed one by one. As usual, Amanda was the last one in the class; she was methodically putting her things away. Claire patiently waited for her. While she tried to hurry, Amanda asked, "How do the rest of you manage to clear off your desks so fast?"

M. Gréfort—one of her favorite teachers—started to grumble as he was rummaging through his papers. This wasn't like him. Amanda looked up. "What's wrong, Monsieur Gréfort?"

"Well!" he exclaimed, "I don't understand. No! I don't get it."

"Can I help you with anything?"

"Where's that paper? Where did that paper go?"

Amanda sighed. Obviously, it wasn't her business. M. Gréfort was so upset that he began to talk out loud again. "With all that, I had hardly prepared my lecture for today!"

"Your lecture was very interesting, as usual," Amanda remarked wholeheartedly.

"I received a paper on which was mentioned that they were going to come to my class this morning to immunize, and then . . . Here it is!"

Amanda held her breath.

"No, I made a mistake. It's next Friday!"

"But they've already immunized."

"Maybe, but there's a second round—for people who were not there; I don't know why. Well, in any case, the mistake is on my part. It's next week."

Amanda finally buckled her bag. The two girls walked out. "Au revoir, Monsieur Gréfort! . . . Claire?"

"Oui?"

"What a shame! It just happens that next week I won't be here on Friday."

* * *

A couple of weeks later, in philosophy class, Amanda stood by the board. It was her turn to present the theme of her choice. She wrote in capital letters: DEATH.

I. LIFE AND DEATH

A. The Death of the Universe

She looked at her classmates. "Death can be presented as a very general physical phenomenon which is not specific to the living being but which concerns, in a larger sense, any closed system . . ."[18]

For the most part, Amanda treated her subject in a philosophical manner. As she came close to the end though, she gave her presentation a new twist.

"The meditation on death is necessary. It helps us understand the value of life. Can we then find some philosophic serenity, affirm that death gives life its significance by putting an end to it? This doesn't bring any solution to the mortal condition of man. Is there a solution? It seems that the answer of philosophy is no (Class book)."

Once she had established her point, she wrote on the board:

III. DOES RELIGION GIVE A SOLUTION?

Then, Amanda entered into a third dimension.

"However, history gives us another point of view. Man didn't need philosophy to start asking questions about death. What are his answers? They belong to the sacred and lead us inevitably to the religious domain.

"Religions contain different doctrines and ways of coping. Religions offer ways to reach heaven, starting from the earth.

[18]Readers will find Amanda's complete presentation in the Annex.

Coming from man, no one can pretend with assurance to hold the truth. However, there is one exception that came down from heaven to earth—from God to man. This religion, different from the others in its very nature, is the revelation of the good news in the person of Jesus Christ. The founders of the other great religions presented themselves as mere human beings and thought of themselves that way. Buddha said at the end of his life, 'I'm still searching for the truth.'

"Christ, according to his own claim, is the Son of God and said, 'I am the truth.' If we want to find answers to our questions—'Why death? Why are we born to die?'—the best way is to turn to Christianity and to the Bible. The Bible takes us back to the creation. The beginnings of man are recorded in the three first chapters of Genesis, the first book of the Bible.[19]

"In Genesis chapter one, death is not spoken of yet. Everything is beautiful and good for man.

"However, Ecclesiastes 7:29 tells us, 'Behold, I have found only this, that God made men upright, but they have sought out many devices.'

"In Genesis chapter two, God warns man of a danger. For the first time in the Bible, we find the mention of death. God also grants man full freedom of choice between life and death.

"In Genesis chapter three, in the Garden of Eden, Adam's choice is called sin. It is the cause of death.

"Romans 5:12 tells us, 'Therefore, just as through one man sin entered into the world, and death through sin, and so death spread to all men, because all sinned . . .'

---

[19]All Scriptures mentioned in this chapter are taken from the New American Standard Bible published by Zondervan.

"In the Bible, God defines sin in the Ten Commandments and in other laws.

"James 4:17 says, 'Therefore, to one who knows the right thing to do and does not do it, to him it is sin.'

"In 1 John 3:4, we learn that 'Everyone who practices sin also practices lawlessness; and sin is lawlessness.'

"Is every man a sinner?

"Genesis 8:21 says, 'The Lord said to Himself, "I will never again curse the ground on account of man, for the intent of man's heart is evil from his youth."'

"Psalm 14:1 says, 'The fool has said in his heart, "There is no God."'

"Proverbs 20:9 says, 'Who can say, "I have cleansed my heart, I am pure from my sin"?'

"Ecclesiastes 7:20 says, 'Indeed, there is not a righteous man on earth who continually does good and who never sins.'

"Isaiah 64:7 says, 'There is no one who calls on Your name, who arouses himself to take hold of You; for You have hidden Your face from us, and have delivered us into the power of our iniquities.'

"The Bible doesn't only convince us of sin and therefore of death. It also gives us a solution to death.

"Romans 6:23 says, 'For the wages of sin is death, but the free gift of God is eternal life in Christ Jesus our Lord.'"

⋆ ⋆ ⋆

Amanda was finished. She picked up her papers and went back to her seat. The class was silent as the teacher evaluated Amanda's presentation. The students were always curious to know the results of someone else's work.

Finally, the teacher looked up. “Good job, Amanda,” she congratulated her. “The subject was treated in an unusual manner.”

Amanda exhaled with relief. Jocelyne smiled at her. She waited for the end of the class to approach to Amanda. “I liked your presentation. It is true that I wouldn’t have treated this subject in the same manner. You know what—that gave me hope! Actually, I’d like to talk more about it.”

Amanda smiled back at her. The two young ladies slowly slipped into a spiritual conversation.

WANTED

THAT EVENING WHILE LOUISE WAS preparing supper, Amanda sat in a corner of the kitchen and read aloud. "Infirmary, March 18, 1980. During the control of the B.C.G. made in the month of November 1979 by the national service of B.C.G., you chose to be controlled by your family doctor. Please send us your certificate before Monday, March 24, 1980, or we will have to give you an intra-dermal reaction here. (We remind you that the B.C.G. immunization is mandatory.) The doctors of the school will be in the building on Tuesday, March 25, from 10 a.m. to 12 noon; the I.D.R. will be done in the classrooms."

"Boy!" she exclaimed. "They are obstinate."

"Who gave you this?" her mother asked.

"My philosophy teacher."

"At least, this time, they told you the day and the time."

"They did, not like the last time in social studies. They acted treacherously, but it didn't work. It's a miracle I was able to get through that one." She added anxiously, "I wish Papa would go talk to them, but I know he doesn't have any time left after he visits Mamie[20] every day at the retirement home. I'd like them to forget me. I'll still have to

---

[20]Mamie is Armand Vissac's mother.

miss some classes. Without mentioning that, some day they might catch me!"

"Don't worry! Up to now, everything has been all right."

"I don't know; the nurse threatened I might not be able to take my baccalauréat exams."

"This is nonsense. As far as I know, they don't ask for immunization papers at the entrance to the examination rooms. Besides, God is with you, isn't He?"

Amanda relaxed. "You're right. God is with me."

* * *

Spring and its budding trees were on the way. The temperature had warmed up and the students headed to their classrooms without any hurry. Amanda entered the school building, which was shaped like a huge rectangular box. She walked up the stairs. Her class was on the second floor. The door to her classroom was about midway down the corridor. It was still locked. As she was waiting with her classmates for the German teacher to arrive, Emma, her tenth-grade old friend passed by. "Emma!"

Emma turned around, "Amanda! What are you doing here?"

"I'm waiting for my teacher, of course! But it's been at least one year since I last saw you. Where are you going like this?"

"I'm going to my class, of course!"

"Where's your class?"

"Over there, right at the end of the corridor."

"I'll accompany you. Just tell me, how come we've never met yet on this floor when our classrooms are so close?"

"I suppose it's because I usually come up the other way."

The young ladies had arrived in front of Emma's room.

"You are right; there is a stairwell here as well. I guess I've never used it. But tell me! How are you doing? How are your studies?"

"Everything is going well."

"Do you still want to be a chiropractor?"

Emma smiled widely, like she used to. "More than ever. It's the most beautiful job in the whole wide world! And what about you?"

"Literature has been wonderful for me. I really feel at ease in that domain."

"What are you going to do later? Have you decided yet?"

"Not really, but now I play the viola. I'm going to the Conservatoire de Versailles."

Suddenly, Amanda jumped back to reality. "Look!" she exclaimed. "The corridor is empty. Everybody is in class." She checked her watch. "My goodness! It's ten minutes past the time. This has never happened to me before."

"To chat too much?" Emma teased her. "I doubt it. But kiss me good-bye before you go. I'm so glad we got to meet!"

"Sure! Next time, let's look for each other so we can talk more."

As Amanda leaned toward Emma to kiss her, she spotted, from the corner of her eye, a white uniform identifying someone who had just entered the second floor at the far end of the corridor.

"Oh my," she whispered to Emma. "I think it's for me."

"What?"

Amanda stooped down to pick up her school bag and, forbidding herself any more glances at the stranger who was fast approaching, she quickly turned her back on her.

"Nothing. Just get in. We're late. I think I'll take a short cut to my class."

Without waiting any longer, she disappeared down the nearby stairs. As she came out, she tried to catch her breath. Slowly she went around the building and followed the walls—hopelessly smooth—looking for a hiding place among the few meager bushes that were growing alongside them. Amanda looked around. At this time, the school grounds were absolutely empty. She came close enough to the other entryway to be able to watch it, hid behind one of the thickest bushes, and waited, her heart beating wildly. She didn't have to wait long. The tap-tap of high heels resounded. The sounds moved to the other side of the building toward the infirmary and faded away. Amanda quickly slipped from her hiding place and succeeded in getting a last glance of the back of the white uniform. She hesitated, then smiled mischievously and entered the school building. She climbed back up the stairs, arrived out of breath at the door of her classroom, and knocked.

"Come in!"

"Excusez moi, monsieur. I'm sorry to be so awfully late."

"Amanda! Here you are! Wait, don't sit down yet."

Without listening to him, Amanda sat down.

"The nurse just left from here, and she's quite upset because she said she has been searching for you for months. Each time it seems that you've been absent. I assured her that you are punctual in class but . . . well, if you could just go right away to the infirmary, I believe this would reassure her a lot."

"Please, monsieur!" Amanda groaned. "There's no emergency. You know . . . it's probably some administrative papers, and I'm already so late! I don't want to miss the whole class for that."

"It's fine with me. You are serious, and I appreciate that. I agree with you, but don't forget to go there as soon as the class is finished."

"Just don't worry, monsieur!" she sighed.

⋆ ⋆ ⋆

One week later, Amanda's classmates who were learning Italian ran up to her like a flight of birds. "Amanda!"

"What is it?"

"The nurse is looking for you everywhere! She came to search for you in our Italian class!"

"But I've never studied Italian!"

"This is what we told her, so she went to see if you were in the Greek class."

Amanda bit her lip so as not to laugh. "Poor lady. I'm giving her such a hard time that she's losing her mind!"

"But what's her problem with you?"

"Well, one should ask her!"

"You'd better go ask her right now, then."

Amanda shrugged and answered lightly, "Maybe." Her eyes twinkled. She had just turned eighteen, and she was not immunized yet!

SWEET CELEBRATION

THE MONTH OF JUNE WAS filled with important final examinations, which led to the obtaining of the baccalauréat diploma, the conclusion of three years of high school studies.

At the Conservatoire de Versailles on the examination day, the five students of M. Villemin waited for their turn. This year, Cédric was one of them. He was to pass the certificate examination for his past year of studies in viola. The certificate year was the highest level, and he would be the last. M. Villemin opened the door for Amanda to enter. She played the allegro of Diptyque by Pierre Lantier. It required prodigious speed. When she stopped, her teacher nodded slightly in an approving manner. She walked out. Véronique was waiting for her. She whispered, "I've never heard you play that piece so fast before."

"I hope it's a good sign. We were supposed to play it as fast as possible. At least this piece didn't leave me any chance to shake."

M. Villemin invited Véronique in. He smiled to Amanda. When Véronique came out, Cédric came forward. He wiped his sweaty hands on his pants. The door opened again. M. Villemin winked to him. As soon as he was in, the two young ladies moved quietly behind the door. They didn't want to miss one single note of Vieux's Concerto. It was beautiful.

* * *

A month later, La Serpe was celebrating the 14th of July, and it was a hot day. Louise and Amanda Vissac cut their way between the crowd and the stands of pralines. They arrived at the salon de thé, downtown.

Louise glanced inside. "There are still some seats," she said. "Come on, ma chérie, let's go in. We'll celebrate your results, the two of us together."

They ordered some ice cream and sat in a cool and quiet corner. Louise said, "That's it! You passed your baccalauréat[21]!"

"That was a real task."

"And now you are an adult."

"And not immunized yet!"

They laughed with joy. Amanda had many reasons to be thankful to God.

"You got a first medal in viola," her mother went on.

"It was a good year. Véronique passed also. I'm glad. This way, I won't be alone in middle 2 in September. Concerning Cédric, he's going to enter the Conservatoire National de Lyon in September."

"Has he taken the entry exam yet?"

"No, but Monsieur Villemin will give him first priority. I'm sure of that because he is his student and he's good."

"I'm happy for him."

---

[21]Baccalauréat: In France, there is no graduation day. The results of the exams are posted on the gates of the schools and come out in the newspapers. The students receive their diploma in the mail.

"Me too. He was born a musician, and he deserves it."

The two women quietly enjoyed their ice cream.

"You forget I received my BAFA also."

"And you got a part-time job as a school supervisor for September," Louise added. "What are you going to do with all that money?"

"This month of summer camp will pay for the Conservatoire. With the August salary, I intend to get a driver's license. Next, if I can save enough money, I'll buy a car. Meanwhile, I'm going to buy some wool and knit a cardigan for myself."

Louise had a happy smile. "Good," she said with approval in her voice. "Just tell me again what Monsieur Villemin did in order to cure you of your shakes. I didn't quite get it yet."

"It's simple, really. He is the one in charge of choosing the official pieces for the viola examinations for the whole French territory. Usually, there is a slow piece and a fast piece. The slow piece doesn't present much technical difficulty, but it's on the slow piece that the shakes are the worst. So, unprecedented, this year Monsieur Villemin decided that there would be no slow piece. In order to have this accepted, he chose a contemporary piece rather difficult and very fast. He told me, 'I'm sure you'll pass on this one,' and he was right."

"Do you realize that all the other violists of your level had to play this piece because of you?"

"I realize that Monsieur Villemin is not an ordinary man. I just love him!"

DAY-CAMP SUPERVISOR

BÉATRICE WAS THE DIRECTOR OF the August summer camp. All her supervisors were gathered around tables set in the shape of a horseshoe as she began to assign them to different age groups.

"Jo and Patrick, you'll have the junior high kids; Alain and Christiane also. There are two groups of junior high. Is that okay with you?"

"No problem." Jo answered for the four of them.

"Paul and Amanda, the juniors. Karima and Luc, you'll take the other group of juniors. By the way, I want to introduce Karima to you. She is my sister-in-law's sister."

"That is, she is the sister of Bertrand's wife," Jo specified.

Karima smiled. She was a pretty little brunette.

"Luc is our youngest supervisor," Béatrice continued. "He just turned sixteen." She turned to him. "This is why you are going to work with Karima. She's experienced, so don't worry; everything will be all right."

The young man smiled. His delicate face, covered with freckles, didn't seem embarrassed. A blond lock fell right to the edge of his eyes. He jerked it back in one motion of the head, uncovering two mischievous blue eyes that twinkled.

The director went on organizing the groups. When she was finished, each pair of supervisors got together to prepare the first day. Béatrice headed toward Paul and Amanda and pulled up a chair.

"You are going to have a difficult child this month. His name is Michel Siron. Amanda, I put him in your team. If you have any problem with him, let me know. I'll expel him right away."

"All right," Amanda answered. "We'll still try to keep him as long as possible."

"I think he'll be better here than at home," Béatrice remarked soberly. "Now, I'd like the supervisors of the juniors to do some activities all together, like going to the swimming pool together. This is to give Karima a break. You can think of other activities too."

"Béatrice, I'd like to do a project of constructing real rafts. What do you think? At twelve years of age, we can't just offer them trifles. They need to handle real stuff."

"I think it would be great, but you'll just never be able to float your rafts."

"What do you mean?" Amanda protested. "You're underestimating us! I built a raft with my brother when I was younger, and it floated."

"That's not the problem. The law requires that to try them, one of us at least must have a lifesaving certificate, and none of us here has one."

"To try it in a puddle of water? Come on, you know the Saucy Brook! Not even a baby could drown in it."

"Even in the Saucy Brook, I would need a lifeguard. But tell me what material you need. I'll cover you." She suddenly got up and went to visit with the other groups.

Amanda smiled widely.

* * *

On the morning of the first day of the August summer camp, Amanda started by calling the group she was in charge of. Slowly, she read down the list of the ten names, looking at the same time at the smiling faces. "Michel Siron," she called.

A twelve-year-old boy, his nostrils wide open, his mouth arrogant, came close to her and straightened up his whole body, right under her nose. "I am Michel Siron. If you don't know me yet, you'll know me soon."

Truly, one warned supervisor is worth two. Amanda observed him with an unmoved calm and then answered gently. "I'm looking forward to it."

He walked away without adding another word. He seemed to be sensitive to a soft answer.

* * *

Toward the middle of the week, Paul and Amanda gathered their group to go play a game of baseball on the sports ground.

"I'm not coming," Michel declared.

"You're coming just like everyone else," Paul retorted. "It's out of the question to leave you here and even less all by yourself."

Michel recovered his arrogant look of the first day. His eyes hardened. "I don't have to receive any order from you."

"Go back home then!"

"I hate you!"

"Just come tell me this again, in front of me."

Michel came close to him. "I hate you," he repeated and then kicked the supervisor on his shin.

Anger seized Paul. He grabbed the child by his arm and kicked him back on his rear end. The boy struggled furiously. Paul let go of him, but Michel charged again and began to hit him with fists and feet. Amanda was watching, powerless. Paul managed to grab him one more time and dragged him to the director's office, where Michel spent the rest of the afternoon.

* * *

When evening came—once all the children had left the camp—Béatrice came up to Paul and Amanda. "You two, come with me to my office."

The two supervisors followed her and chose each one a chair.

"Well then," she asked, "what do you intend to do with that Michel Siron?"

"Send him back home," Paul answered bluntly. "His behavior is unacceptable."

"Amanda, you are his supervisor. What do you think?"

Amanda was silently thinking. She finally said: "I haven't had any serious personal problems with him yet, therefore I think it wouldn't be honest on my part to send him home."

Béatrice remarked, "He seems to have difficulty essentially with masculine authority. I think you shouldn't take it personally, Paul."

Paul shook his head. "I'm not worried about that. What concerns me most is that he may well spoil the other children's camp experience."

"I don't think so," Amanda pleaded. "When he refuses to play, they are simply happy—and when he agrees to play, it's good for the other children to learn to make an effort to include him in the game. In any case, it can't spoil character."

"Paul," Béatrice concluded, "the best you can do might be to ignore his moods. I think we'll try to give him another chance."

* * *

On Friday, at the end of the first week of day camp, Amanda was walking back from the coffee break when Paul spotted her. He left his post. They exchanged a few words in the middle of the courtyard. "Some are finishing their pottery, and others are making crocodiles with beads. In short, everything is calm. There is nothing worth mentioning."

Paul hurried to the coffee break. When Amanda entered the cool shade of their room, the children had found refuge in the corners and were trying to protect their heads with their arms. The girls were screaming indignantly. At one end of the room, Michel was holding onto leftovers from the pottery clay, which he had shaped into bullets, and he was aiming at the opposite wall, now full of big red marks.

"Michel!"

The boy threw another projectile and raised his arm again. Amanda stood in front of him. "Stop this right now!"

He let his arm down, a mocking smile on his lips. Amanda quickly snatched all the bullets out of his hands and evaluated the disaster. "Well, this is not the end. Now we must clean up."

"I'm not going to clean up."

"If you want to spend the rest of the afternoon in the director's office, it's your choice. And don't forget she could very well send you just right back to your home."

"I don't care." He sighed and started to pick up the clay.

He had barely finished gathering up the globs of red clay when Paul arrived. It was two o'clock, and the activities were starting again. "This afternoon, we're going to play cops and robbers in the woods," he announced. "That way, you can spend your energy in the shade."

The children shouted with enthusiasm. Paul had them stand two by two outside while Amanda was getting the last ones out. Finally, there remained only Michel. "Come on, Michel, we are waiting for you!" she said.

The boy stared at her, seized a box of tiny beads, and without letting go of her gaze, he let the whole content of the box run to the ground. Then, quick as lightning, he grabbed another box and emptied it on the table. Amanda seized his hand. "You won't get out of here before you pick up all of that!"

Paul's head appeared in the door. "Are you coming?"

"Michel is behaving silly. He'll have to pick up these beads before he goes. Can you wait for us a few more minutes?"

"Say, Amanda, it's hot here outside. I'm going to take the other kids to the woods. You catch up with us as soon as you're finished."

"I'm sorry to leave you by yourself."

"Don't worry for that!" Paul insisted. "I'd rather be with the nineteen others than with him. Besides, it's not fair that everybody should wait for Mister Michel. Actually, just take your time and don't worry; we'll be all right. We'll be just fine."

"All right," Amanda said with a sigh. "Anyway, I don't have much choice."

The group left. Michel had not touched one single bead yet. "Come on, my boy, get to work!"

Slowly, one by one, Michel started by picking up the beads that were on the table. Then, he sat on the ground and began to gather the ones that were on the floor. During that time, Amanda was putting away the other boxes. When she saw he was coming to the end, she bent down to give him a hand. He then stared at her and, with a wide smile, seized the two boxes of the beads he had just picked up, one in each hand, and threw them up in the air in a colorful rain.

Amanda bent toward him and quickly, without thinking, hit him on his bare thigh. He straightened up, like a wounded animal, raised his fist right above his head and aimed at her face. She stopped breathing. The hard gaze of the boy crossed her tender eyes. "I'm sorry," she said softly, "I didn't mean to hit you, but you asked for it."

Slowly, he let his arm down.

"Michel, we've got to pick up these beads. I'm going to help you."

The calm response of his supervisor seemed to have a soothing effect on him. Without a word, he started to pick up beads again. This time, she kept the boxes in her hand. When they were finished, one hour had gone by.

"Michel, I've got to talk to you. I owe Paul an explanation for our absence, and he's waiting for the first opportunity to have you expelled. To tell the truth, it can't go on like this. I don't have the right to abandon the rest of the team for you. Today is an exception, but it can't happen again. I can only try to support you if you promise you won't do this again and if you make an effort to behave."

As she was talking, they had come out to the front of their prefab room. Its shade was now sufficient for them to shelter from the sun. Amanda was facing the boy, but he remained silent, looking to the ground. "Maybe you'd rather not come back?" she asked.

He shook his head and looked at her. His eyes had strangely softened. "Amanda, I'd love to promise you to behave, but . . ." He stopped. She waited. He swallowed hard.

"Well, tell me! What's holding you from doing it?" she encouraged him gently.

His face was absolutely serious. He was not recognizable. "I'm afraid I can't do it."

"Michel! I'm not asking you to be perfect. All I'm asking is for you to try, to do your best. What do you think?"

He nodded. "All right, then."

Paul and the other children were coming back from the sports ground.

* * *

That evening, Paul asked if they could meet in Béatrice's office. "The joke has lasted long enough," he started.

"What happened?" Béatrice asked.

Briefly, Amanda told the incident of the beads without getting into the more dramatic details. She concluded, "I agree with Paul. This can't happen again."

"What do you intend to do then?"

"I've already talked to Michel. I asked him to promise me to behave from now on, or I won't be able to help him."

"Don't tell me that he promised you!" Paul exclaimed.

“No . . . actually, he did better than that.” Amanda was taking her time. She had Paul and Béatrice’s full attention.

“He’s been honest, and that touched me.”

“Explain!” Béatrice ordered.

“He said he’d love to promise but he was afraid he couldn’t hold to his promise. Therefore, he committed himself to try to behave, and I believe he was serious about it.”

“Well!” Béatrice commented.

Paul sighed. “All right.”

Amanda was about to get up when Béatrice stopped her. “Just a minute, you two. I want to give you one word of advice. In the case you should hold different opinions, don’t deal with your differences in front of the children.”

Paul and Amanda looked at each other. “I won’t,” Paul said.

“I think we’ve been doing okay so far,” his colleague remarked.

COUSCOUS[22] PARTY

THE DAY-CAMP CENTER HAD JUST let out. Amanda went back to the concrete schoolyard where they had spent some time that afternoon skateboarding. She checked to make sure they hadn't left anything behind; she picked up a board. On her way back, as she was walking across a grass field, she started to sing the song she had just been teaching the children at the end of the day:

"Let me go back to my prairie
Let me see again the vast horizons
The feverish gallop—"

She stopped dead. A missile had just landed in front of her. Another one reached her calf. She turned around and scrutinized the surroundings. The field was absolutely empty. There was only a thickly leafed apple tree standing in its middle. She slowly drew close to it. A rain of green apples welcomed her. She used her arms as a shield to protect her face. The branches of the tree moved.

"Hey, up there," she shouted. "When the geese are perched, it means good weather!"

---

[22]Couscous is the North African national dish made of semolina, vegetables, and meat.

Nimble as a cat, Luc, the young supervisor, eyes shiny, let himself land by her side. "Tell me, are you going to be here tomorrow night?"

"What's happening tomorrow night?"

"We're having a party."

"It's not the end of the month though."

"Who cares? We'll have another one at the end of the month. Karima wants to make couscous for all the supervisors. It's nice, isn't it! So, are you going to come?"

"Why not? It's really kind of her. I'm surely not going to let you eat the couscous all by yourselves. I'll tell my parents tonight that I'll be back late tomorrow evening."

As they talked, they arrived at the main courtyard. Paul was busy in front of the cabin, putting away tools and boards as he sang: "It's a famous three masts, fine like a bird, hissé-ho! Santiago. . ."

Béatrice passed by, smiling. She stopped in front of the rafts that were taking shape. "So," she said, "I haven't heard about Michel Siron this week."

"It's been quiet these days," Paul answered.

"May it last!" Jo threw in, as she was joining in.

The telephone rang in Béatrice's office. "Jo, can you answer while I'm going around? It's probably for Karima."

"I'll go get her," Luc offered right away.

They scattered, each one going his way.

* * *

The next evening, the supervisors hurried to finish their daily cleaning. Béatrice came out of the office. "I'm leaving," she announced.

"Already?" Amanda exclaimed.

"The couscous is ready! Hurry up. It has to be eaten hot."

"Won't you stay?" Jo asked.

"Non," Béatrice replied. "You need to spend some time without me. Jo, please, I count on you to lock everything behind you." She handed her a bunch of keys. Jo took them and headed toward the junior high's tent. Patrick was coming out of it. The telephone in the office rang. "I'm going to answer it!" he quickly offered. He grabbed the keys from Jo's hand and covered the short distance that separated him from the office with long strides. Amanda went back into her room.

"It looks good," Paul declared. "It's finished."

"I've still got to sweep the floor. I'll join you all as soon as I'm done," Amanda replied.

"Leave that for once!"

"I have the bad habit of always being the last one, and I can't break myself from this," she grumbled as she headed out to get the broom.

* * *

When Amanda finished sweeping the room and stepped outside, not a single supervisor was in sight. The temperature had suddenly dropped, and thick fog covered the compound, making it difficult for her to find her way to the door of the dining room. She heard a car start and pull away. As she stepped into the dining room, a delicious aroma welcomed her. It was warm inside, and most of the supervisors were there. The table was set. The couscous was steaming on the stove, but it was unusually quiet. She looked around. "Where's Karima?" she asked.

"She just left!" Luc answered.

"Did she forget something?"

"No," Luc answered again.

"Are we going to eat Karima's couscous without her? What happened? What's going on?"

"Amanda, you've just asked all the wrong questions," Jo muttered.

"Just don't try to understand," Paul added.

"Wait a minute! The couscous is here, and Karima is not. What's the story? I'm telling you, I'm not going to eat that couscous without her until I know what happened."

"She's got a point," Jo said.

"It's her father's fault!" Patrick exclaimed.

"Her father's fault? Didn't he know she was making couscous?"

"Oh, he knew! It's been planned for a while."

"Her father is annoying," Luc explained. "Every day he calls to check on her—to find out if she's arrived safely or if she's still on the way. In a word, he doesn't give her any space. I see it. I'm working with her."

"So he wanted her to go back home?"

"No, she wanted to go back home!" Alain said.

"Wait a minute," Jo interrupted, "I'm going to tell you the whole story." Jo had a natural authority. When she spoke, everyone listened.

"It's true that Karima's father calls her every evening, and it has been annoying to everyone, especially Patrick and Luc. So Patrick decided to play a trick on him tonight. When her father called, Patrick went to answer the phone. Instead of calling Karima, however, he told her father some silly things—like his daughter wasn't here, and you can imagine what. Then he hung up. When Karima learned this, she got very upset and left. She said it wasn't being respectful to her father. That's what she said."

Patrick had turned his back on them. He was at the window, trying to pierce through the fog.

"I understand her," Amanda said simply.

The young man sharply turned around. "What do you mean, you understand her! A father that sticky, it just can't be! I don't regret one minute what I did, except that Karima got upset."

"Maybe she doesn't find her father sticky after all. Maybe she loves him. Actually, that would be rather normal."

"No! Her father is not normal," Luc stepped in.

"She's over twenty. At that age, it's too much," Patrick continued.

"There's no age limit for being a daughter or for loving as a father."

"This is not love," Patrick argued. "He's controlling her, and she can't even breathe."

"My father has a tendency to worry about me too, and I'm glad for it. It's his way of loving me."

"Amanda, stop it!" Jo ordered suddenly.

Amanda stared at her with surprise. "Did I say anything wrong?"

"Just be quiet," Christiane repeated, without any other word of explanation.

Amanda obeyed and went around the table. Luc had his back to the door. But he hadn't given up yet. "Parents are useless!" he provoked her with rage. "Except to keep us from living our life!"

"Parents are useful because they love us," Amanda insisted calmly.

"This isn't true," he persisted; "Actually, parents—we can very well do without them. We don't need them."

Amanda turned back toward him: "Luc, how can you say that?"

"Amanda!" Jo tried to remind her.

"I say it, and I maintain it," Luc insisted.

"But, Luc," Amanda said softly, "You know how it is, don't you? Don't you too have parents?"

A dead silence fell on the room. Everyone was holding his breath. Luc became terribly pale. Slowly, he raised his hands, in a gesture of surrender. He swallowed painfully and managed to say in a strangled voice. "All right, Amanda, I yield."

"But . . ."

He took a step backward. "No, no, I give up." He suddenly turned around, opened the door that was behind him, and disappeared into the fog.

A HARD TRUTH

LITTLE BY LITTLE, EVERYONE WAS breathing again.

"You won!" Jo exclaimed.

"Well . . . what's going on?" Amanda asked, perplexed.

"Don't you realize what you've done?" Alain said threateningly.

"No, she doesn't know," Jo answered.

"She'd better not! And next time, shut your big mouth," he rudely advised.

"Remember, we told you to be quiet!" Christiane reproached.

"You can't force me to be quiet regarding what I don't know," Amanda retorted defensively.

There was silence.

"Obviously that's right," Jo said. "Everyone here knows the facts but Amanda. We should have told her earlier."

Patrick nodded. "You tell her!"

"Luc is an orphan," Jo announced solemnly.

"What?"

"God knows what he's doing now," Christiane whispered.

Amanda opened her mouth, closed it, and resolutely walked to the door. Patrick quickly strode from the window to the entrance and blocked her way. "Where are you going?"

"Let me through."

"No way! First tell me where you are going."

Alain drew close on the other side. She thought rapidly. "I'm going out." She glanced toward the window to her left. Patrick followed her eyes and moved slightly that way. Quick as lightning, she slipped around him to the right, grabbed the doorknob, and escaped. She was barely outside when Alain darted out and caught up with her. He grabbed her right arm and turned her around to face him. "Didn't you hear what we said?"

"Let me go!" she begged. She tried to free herself but quickly stopped. The young man was too strong for her. He dragged her roughly back inside the room. "What are we going to do to her to teach her a lesson? Lock the entryway and the exit, and keep the keys safe," he ordered.

Christiane rushed to the bunch of keys, which Jo had left on the table, while other supervisors took position quickly by the window and the two doors. As Christiane was trying all the keys feverishly on the safety exit, Amanda looked around. Only Jo hadn't moved from her chair.

"Could you lessen your grip?"

"Don't you even try it! You are not going to get out of here!"

She clenched her teeth. Alain read the anxiety in her eyes. He kept his grip tight. She drew in her breath and regained some confidence. "All right, I made a mistake. Let me at least try to repair it."

"What do you intend to do for that?" he questioned harshly.

"You really want to know?"

"I do!"

"Well then, let go of me first!"

Knowing that all the exits were guarded, he finally released her. She rubbed her arm.

"So?"

"I'm going to apologize!"

He examined her from head to toe while the others gazed around disconcertedly. "Let her go!" Jo ordered suddenly.

After some hesitation, they freed the way. "What a shame!" Alain exclaimed. "I wish we had a special party for you."

Amanda glanced thankfully toward her old friend and, without waiting any longer, stepped into the mist.

* * *

She began by going meticulously around the buildings. There was not so much as a cat to be seen. The campgrounds were spacious and in the fog, it was impossible to see more than two meters in front of her. "Lord, help me!" she prayed.

She headed toward the woods. Thanks to the trees, visibility there was better. She skirted around the inner grove, trying to pierce each corner. Once convinced that no one was there, she came back to the edge of the wood and stopped in front of the cottony wall, indecisive. "Luc!" she called softly.

Suddenly, in front of her, the shape of the boy appeared, coming like out of the clouds. He was anxiously drawing on a cigarette. His nerves seemed to run right under his skin. He avoided her eyes—his glance, usually so joyful, drowned in the mist.

"Luc, I'm sorry . . . I didn't know. They just told me . . . Would you please forgive me?"

He drew another puff; his hand was trembling. He finally said in a hoarse voice. "I think I needed to hear what you said."

She tried to draw closer, but he stopped her with a gesture of the hand. "No, stay where you are." He turned his back on her, moved a few steps away, and then stopped. He was struggling to keep control of himself. She didn't move.

"I'd rather know the truth . . . even if it's hard to hear. Later, it can be useful." He slowly turned around. He saw the tense look on her face. Each was as pale as the other. "Don't worry, it'll pass," he reassured her gently.

"The others are concerned about you. Are you coming in? What should I tell them?"

He nodded. "I need to calm down. I'm going to have another smoke, and then I'll come in."

Amanda walked to him and warmly squeezed his arm. "See you soon then. We'll be waiting for you."

In return, he gave her a weak smile.

* * *

When Amanda entered the living room, no one had moved from his place. The concern was obvious. "So?" Jo wondered.

"He needs to smoke a little longer, and then he'll join us," Amanda replied.

"How is he doing?"

"He'll be all right."

Nobody dared to ask any more questions. "As far as I'm concerned," Amanda added, "I suggest we heat up the couscous while we're waiting for him."

Everyone agreed to that.

* * *

The next day, the two groups of juniors were going together to the swimming pool.

"I can't swim. I'll stay on the side to watch," Karima proposed.

Paul and Luc plunged right in. Paul decided to lead a group in a length competition. Karima brought out two huge rubber skiffs. "Here, Luc, catch these. You can use them to play pirates."

Amanda had barely settled into one of the boats when Luc overturned it. He was swimming like a fish. Two teams quickly formed and engaged in boat grappling. Luc and Amanda were the undisputed captains of the "ships." When all the "sailors" were at sea, Luc let out a savage scream and jumped on the enemy ship, attempting to throw its captain out. Sometimes Amanda tried to resist, to the great joy of her team; sometimes she jumped in the water at the arrival of her enemy and reappeared, victorious, on his abandoned ship.

Karima called, "Luc, it's time to come out. I'm going to the girls' cabins. Paul is already with the boys. Would you and Amanda go around the pool to bring everyone in?"

The two captains obeyed. Luc swam quickly to the edge of the pool and pulled himself up. Amanda followed more slowly, checking that there were no more known faces around her. When she got to the edge, all their children were out of the water. Luc bent forward and extended a hand out to her. His eyes glittered mischievously. She refused the help. “You are going to throw me back into the water.”

“No,” he insisted, “I promise you.”

With hesitation, she accepted his hand. He grinned. “This is so you can forgive me for all the water you’ve drunk today because of me.”

They went around the pool, chasing after their children, and met back at the entrance to the cabins. “Luc?”

“Yes?”

“I would have loved to have a younger brother like you!”

She disappeared into the women’s section. The boy remained a few seconds, motionless, before disappearing in his turn.

AMANDA'S SECRET

FOR THE JUNIORS, THE NEXT day was a big day. The rafts were finished. Béatrice let them out in the woods, by the side of a trail that led to Saucy Brook. "I'll come back for you at four thirty exactly. Be ready!"

The group carried the rafts down to the bank and laid them at the edge of the water. Paul stepped down into the creek and went to explore. "The brook is navigable for about twenty meters. In some places, it's as deep as my waist, but no more."

"This is perfect!" his colleague answered.

The rafts floated. The children spent the afternoon taking turns floating up and down the stream. Except for Michel, who was sometimes grumpy, the time went by too fast. The activity was a great success, and at four o'clock Amanda had a hard time gathering the troop even for chocolate bars. As time was moving on, she proposed, "I'm going to start to bring the rafts back to the road. Who will help me?"

A few children got up right away and followed her on the trail. They had just put the rafts down when a girl came running toward them. "Amanda, come quick!"

"What's wrong?"

"There's a fight!"

"Paul is back there, isn't he?"

"I'm telling you to come!"

Amanda hurried back to the brook. A pack of children were stacked up on top of each other. A few meters from there, Paul was watching them, laughing.

"Michel is at the bottom of the pile," her informer said.

Amanda swiftly moved closer. "Get up!"

They were so tangled up that it seemed impossible to separate them. She grabbed the boy who was on the top of the heap. "Paul said we could!" he protested.

"And I'm saying it's enough!" she ordered severely.

One by one, the children got up. Finally, she saw the bottom of the knot. Michel lay there on his back, his arms folded over his face. He didn't move. She quickly removed the last fighters and bent toward him. Gently, she opened his arms. He was crying. "Come on, get up," she said while helping him.

He obeyed but kept covering his face. As soon as he stood up, he turned to them, his face smeared with tears. "I hate you. I hate you all." He turned around and fled, running into the woods.

"Michel!" his supervisor called.

She was about to go after him when Paul stopped her, holding her by the arm. "I warn you, Amanda, as soon as Béatrice arrives, I'll ask for his immediate expulsion!"

The children were quiet. Michel was running away. She stared at the serious faces turned toward her. "Please, behave for a minute," she implored. "I must talk with Paul."

They walked a few meters away. "Do you realize that what you were doing is illegal?" she reproached him sternly.

"And do you realize that though you're responsible for this child, he doesn't obey you when you call him back?"

"No wonder, after the treatment he received!"

"All right. Go after him now. I bet you won't even be able to bring him back."

"Paul," she said slowly, "if I should bring him back before the arrival of Béatrice, I don't want to hear you talk about expelling him until the end of camp—and I'll be quiet about this."

"And if Béatrice gets back before you?"

"He'll be sent home, obviously, but you can be sure she'll learn about everything that happened today!" she threatened.

"That's fine with me," he said.

She took off running. She couldn't see any trace of the boy anywhere. The path made a bend. After the turn, she noticed him in the far distance, sitting on the edge of the trail. "Michel, come back!" she shouted.

As soon as he heard her, he got up and bolted straight ahead. Suddenly, he turned to the right onto a goats' trail that reached up into the void. A few minutes later, Amanda climbed up the same way. The path was difficult. Stones were rolling under her feet. Finally, she saw the boy again. He was sitting on the rocky path, his head in his arms. She dropped down next to him, exhausted. Slowly, she recovered her breath. "Come on, Michel, we have to go back."

"No, I don't want to."

"Béatrice is coming soon."

"I don't care."

"I can't leave you here in the woods all by yourself."

"I don't want to see them ever again. Never! I hate them all."

He wiped his face with the back of his hand. She laid her arm around his shoulders. "I'll be with you." She got up. "Come on, let's go."

"No!"

Amanda waited a little longer, silently. What to do? She looked at the side of the way that was going back down, then slowly turned around and decided to continue to walk up. Several meters away, she came upon railroad tracks. On the other side stood a huge boulder, shaped like a sphere, sitting in the middle of an empty clearing.

She crossed over the tracks, went around the rock, and leaned on it. "Lord," she prayed, "I'm at my wits' end. Please, help me."

She had just finished praying when she heard, "Amanda!"

She held her breath. Michel's voice called again. He had just come out onto the train tracks. She heard him cross over and draw near the rock. While he was going around it she glided, with the silence of the Sioux, along its wall so as not to be seen. The child left. He called one more time. This time, his voice was pressing. "Amanda, where are you? Come back!"

At the sound of the rolling stones, she could tell he had started back down. She smiled. She waited a little longer, made sure he was out of sight, and without hurry, trailed after him. The boy had nearly come to the main path when she found him sitting in the gravel. She walked up to him and said simply, "Come on, let's go!"

He got up. "Where were you?"

"That's my secret."

She put her hand on his collar and gently pushed him forward. He didn't resist. The others had left the riverbank. Amanda and

Michel followed the way that led to the road. She saw with relief that Béatrice's vehicle hadn't arrived yet. She kept her protégé next to her. "What's going on?" she asked Paul.

"Béatrice is over fifteen minutes late."

Just at that time, the van appeared.

"So?" Amanda said.

"You win," Paul answered, as a good player.

* * *

Back at the center, the children scattered right away. After Paul and Amanda had finished their cleaning session, the young lady decided to stop by the tent of the junior highs. Jo was there, singing a lullaby to herself:

"Doucement, doucement, doucement s'en va le jour.

Doucement, doucement, à pas de velours."[23]

Amanda joined in. "The warbler has said its night song.

The hare has fled without a sound."

As soon as she saw Amanda, Jo smiled. Two dimples appeared on her cheeks. "Come close!" she ordered in her usual gruff manner. She lowered her voice. "You know what?"

"I don't, but I have the feeling I will soon."

Jo's eyes were laughing. "Béatrice is demanding that Patrick apologize to Karima's father."

Amanda nodded. "That's good," she said simply.

"I heard that Luc wanted to apologize to Karima too. Of course, she wasn't peeved with him."

Amanda remarked, "He's a very special boy."

---

[23]"Softly, softly, softly the day is leaving. Softly, softly, with velvety steps."

"By the way, I won't be able to take you home tonight. My car is full. I asked Alain to do it, and he's agreed."

Amanda made a face.

"Does it bother you? Well then, if you want, I'll come back to get you," Jo offered.

"No," Amanda protested, "I can't criticize his way of driving before I've tried it."

The dimples reappeared. "He's a bit of a buckaroo, but I'm sure you'll come out of it."

Amanda sighed and left the tent. Alain was waiting for her. She climbed into the passenger's seat, buckled her belt, and sank deeply into her place as well as into silence. As soon as they left the town limits, the young man pressed the accelerator to the floor of the car. Just before the turns, he would brake abruptly at the last minute, then take the turn in a noisy squealing of tires and press the accelerator to the floor again. Suddenly, he slowed down and observed the girl next to him. "Aren't you afraid?" he asked.

"No, why? Am I supposed to be?"

"Do you know what speed we are traveling at?"

"Do you?"

"130[24]."

"Are you afraid?"

"Non!"

"Do you know what you are doing?"

"Ouais!"

"Well then, there is no reason for me to be afraid. You are holding the wheel, aren't you? And if I were afraid, would it change anything?"

---

[24]The speed is in kilometers/hour.

"Non!"

She sank back into her muteness.

"Do you know you're abnormal!" he exclaimed with his customary rudeness.

"Let's say I'm different," she corrected him.

"You can say so!"

They had come to her home.

* * *

The month of August was drawing to an end. Paul, Amanda, and the children were coming back on bicycles from an overnight campout. Amanda was bringing up the rear, having made sure Michel was right in front of her. The little country road was empty. She pushed on her pedals to catch up with him and rode alongside him.

"Amanda," he asked suddenly out of the blue, "do you know the prayer 'Our Father who is in heaven'?"

"Yes, I do."

"You do?" His face brightened. "Do you know it by heart?"

"Yes. Why?"

"I've been looking for it, but I don't know where to find it. Amanda, please, could you write it for me?"

"I'll do it with pleasure."

"You won't forget?"

"As soon as we're back at the center, I'll write it for you," she promised.

When they arrived, the compound was closing its gates. A few parents were still waiting for the children who were just pulling in. Michel dropped his bicycle to the ground. Nobody was here for him; he usually went back home alone. He hurried inside the center. "Amanda, wait for me," he shouted. "I'll be back in a minute."

She went in to meet him. He was already coming back with a piece of white paper and a pen in his hand. "Here, Amanda, write my prayer."

She applied herself to it and then underlined the words "forgive us our trespasses as we forgive those who trespass against us" and "deliver us from the evil one." At the bottom, she signed: "With love from your supervisor, Amanda." He was standing next to her, waiting, his knees restlessly moving back and forth with impatience. He was about to tear the paper from her hand, but she held onto it. "Tell me, why are you asking me for this?"

"When I'm at my grandmother's, she recites it with me."

"Good!"

"Now I'll be able to say it all by myself."

Amanda fixed her gaze on him. "I'm going to tell you a secret."

He calmed down all at once and listened with attention.

"I've been praying for you every morning before coming to the center."

He stared at her, speechless.

"Here!" She handed him the paper.

He pulled it out of her hands as if he were a parched land thirsting for rain, and started to read it aloud right away. When he came to the underlined words, he read them slowly, stopped, and looked at his supervisor.

"I underlined them because I think it's important for you," she explained.

Then the last thing she would have expected happened. The arrogant boy of the first day of summer camp blushed like a little girl.

He finished his reading silently, quickly folded the paper, and slid it between his chest and shirt. "Amanda, I'll keep it forever!"

"May God watch over you, gamin[25]!"

He got onto his bicycle. Amanda, lost in her thoughts, watched him ride away pushing energetically on the pedals. Béatrice had come up silently behind her, and she surprised her.

"Did you exchange addresses?" Béatrice asked.

"No."

"Amanda, you did a good job with him."

The young supervisor glanced back at her. "Thanks!" she briefly replied.

---

[25]kid

SCHOOL SUPERVISOR

THE FIRST DAY OF SCHOOL of September 1980, in one of the most important middle schools of La Serpe, Amanda watched the courtyard somewhat nervously. Suddenly, a band of five children appeared in front of her.

"Amanda, do you recognize us?"

The face of the young lady brightened. "Do I recognize you? Of course! We were in day camp together in July! Did you think I would forget you so fast? And just what are you doing here?"

"This is our school!"

"You, I don't know you," she said to one of the boys.

"No, you don't. My name is Thierry. However, they've talked to me about you."

A smile spread on the delicate face of the child. The bell rang.

"It's time to go in. Go get in line."

"We'll see you at recess!" they shouted, leaving.

* * *

That school was notorious for being a hotbed of violence. Children of different cultural backgrounds attended there. One morning after the children had assembled in their classrooms, Amanda entered the supervisors' office. The head supervisor was competent. "Good morning, Amanda. Is everything okay today?" he asked.

She sighed. "There is tension in the air. Out in the yard, the Moroccans were on one side and the Algerians on the other. They were faced off and had daggers drawn. A spark could set a fire. The French kids in the middle didn't quite know where to go."

"I know. It's because of the war in the Sahara. I hope it's not going to explode here. I'll come and help supervise at ten o'clock."

"Good. Thank you!"

* * *

During noon break, a team of older children was playing soccer in the yard. One of them kicked the ball so hard that it disappeared into the neighbor's property. Amanda ran up. The boys were easily a head taller than her. "You!" she pointed to one of them. "I allow you to go get it. Go around to the neighbors, excuse yourself politely, and ask if you can get your ball back."

The boy didn't reply, but instead of heading to the school entrance, he ran toward the heavy wire fence. "You mustn't enter that way!" Amanda shouted.

Without listening, he grasped the fence, climbed over it, and landed in the neighbor's garden. Almost immediately, an enormous guard dog appeared, growling ferociously, and planted its fangs in the boy's calf. He let out a scream of pain. The dog opened its jaw for a splint second. That was enough for the young man to throw himself on the fence and clamber back into the courtyard. Amanda hurried up to him. "Show me the bite!"

"No," he refused, grinning with pain. "I'll be okay."

"Show me the wound!" she repeated firmly. "I'm responsible for you here."

The wound was ugly. "I'm sorry, but I must take you to the infirmary."

The head supervisor came out at that very moment. "What's going on?"

"He was just bitten by the neighbor's dog."

"What was he doing at the neighbor's?"

"He climbed over the fence to go get his ball."

"Why didn't he go around?"

"I asked him to, but he didn't listen to me."

"Very well," said the head supervisor. "I'll take care of him." He turned to the injured youth. "You—come with me."

The boy turned even paler. The head supervisor was noted for severity.

After they had disappeared into the school building, Amanda's little band ran up to her and circled her. "Amanda, we hope you won't have any trouble."

"Trouble? What for?"

"He's going to be punished because of what you said."

"Well, it seems to me he brought it on himself. That might teach him to listen. Come on, don't worry for me; rather, go play."

The children obeyed, but Thierry stayed back with her. His honest, limpid eyes looked up to her. "You know, Amanda, he is part of a gang. The other day they waited for one of the supervisors outside the school because he had punished one of them. They had knives. The police had to intervene. I'm really concerned for you."

She smiled. "I said not to worry. I did my job, and I'm not afraid."

"Aren't you?"

"No, I'm not."

"How come?"

"Well . . ." She hesitated. "You really want to know?"

"Sure!"

"God's with me."

He sighed. "I believe in God too, but I'm upset with Him."

She stared at him, surprised. "Oh!"

He nodded and looked away toward the courtyard. For a minute, they watched the young people run after one another. "Amanda, I'd like to tell you why. But you must promise me first that you won't tell anyone."

"All right. I promise."

"I pray to Him, but He doesn't answer my prayers."

"That's possible. However, God always hears our prayers."

"Why doesn't He answer me then?"

"I suppose it depends on what you're asking Him."

"I'm asking Him for something good." He hesitated. "At home, I have a little brother. He is handicapped, in a wheelchair. I've often asked God to heal him, but so far He never has."

Amanda bit her lip.

"It's surely a good thing," he continued. "Amanda, tell me, why doesn't God answer my prayers? Is He going to heal him someday? Could He be trying to teach me to be patient?"

Amanda was trying to think. "Thierry, God always answers. Only . . . sometimes . . . He says no."

"Do you believe God is good?"

"Yes, I do. He is good."

"Why would He refuse that then?"

She sighed and prayed to God to inspire her with an answer.

"Do you love your little brother?"

"Yes, I do!"

"Do you think you'd love him more if he was healed?"

The child thought for a few seconds. "No, I don't think so."

"Well then, this is what's truly important."

"You mean . . . to love him as he is?"

"Exactly! I believe God doesn't expect anything more from you."

He stared at her intensely. "Some things are so hard to understand!"

"That's right. I don't understand everything either. Sometimes, the only solution is to accept the fact that we don't understand."

The bell rang.

"Amanda, I love you very much."

"I love you too."

SARABANDE

BESIDES WORKING PART TIME AS a school supervisor, Amanda continued to attend the Conservatoire de Musique de Versailles. One Wednesday afternoon in the viola room, her session ended, and she began to put her instrument back in its case.

"Amanda!"

"Oui, monsieur?"

"I must tell you I won't be here next week. However, you'll still have your class. I've asked for someone to replace me."

"All right!"

* * *

The next day, Amanda was posted at the entry gate of the school to observe the departure of the students. There were very few children left, and she was about to leave her place when a fight broke out on the outside of the school grounds. She hesitated. Two medium-size boys were visibly settling a difference. Suddenly she moved out. Two other boys rushed to meet her. "Mademoiselle, this is not in the school. You don't have the right to intervene."

"That's right," she answered coldly, "but here, at least, I have the right to hit!"

The two forerunners rushed back to the fight. "Watch out, boys! The supervisor is coming. She's going to beat you."

She was already on top of them. She seized the two scufflers by their collars and shook them. "That's enough now! Get along to your homes."

The gang quickly dispersed. Amanda smiled, satisfied, and headed for the supervisors' lounge.

* * *

A week later when Amanda stepped in the viola classroom, the substitute was there. He was a tall man—thin and nervous, the exact opposite of M. Villemin. After the usual warm-up exercises, he asked, "What are you working on these days?"

"I'm playing the sarabande of the first suite of Bach."

"All right, go ahead, I'm listening!"

She had barely played two measures when he interrupted her. "Faster, please!"

"This is a largo," she remarked.

"I know, but you can still play it faster."

She laid the bow on the string and started again at the beginning . . . at the same speed.

"I said faster."

She didn't stop but continued at the same rhythm.

"Stop!"

She lifted her bow.

"I want the piece played like this: pam, pam, pam, pam. Do you get it?"

"I do!"

"Your turn, then!"

She began the sarabande again, at the same speed as before. The substitute instructor was beginning to lose patience. He interrupted her again, seized his instrument, and played the first measures. "This is what I want! Do you understand?"

She placed her viola under her chin and played again at her elected speed. Suddenly, the man understood. "That's enough. You are stubborn. Put your instrument away!"

She had not played more than three measures. Without a word, she obeyed and left the room.

* * *

At school, in the supervisors' room, three young people were conversing.

"Amanda, what horror movie have you seen lately?"

"I've seen none so far."

"Impossible!"

"Not only is this possible, but I also feel very good about it."

"You've got to have watched at least one horror movie sometime in your life."

"Really?"

"Absolutely!"

"All right, tell me then what compels you to watch horror movies?"

"I don't know. I do know that afterwards, I can't sleep for about a week. I have nightmares sometimes. I double-lock my door, but I'm still scared that someone might enter—"

"Excuse me, but I don't have the money to spend on that kind of pleasure!"

One of the boys sighed. "All right, Manu, what do you think about us pulling off some magic?"

"Yep! We have one hour to kill. I'm going to get some glasses."

Manu came back with four glasses. He placed them at the four corners of the table, and then sat on one side with his colleague on the other. Amanda observed nervously. "What do you intend to do?"

"We're gonna try to levitate these glasses."

"By blowing on them?"

"Don't be stupid. We've got to concentrate and call on the spirits."

"Have you ever done this before?"

"No, but I've read some books on it, and someone who's done it advised us."

"Come on, let's try! Let's see if it works!"

The two boys became silent and began their meditation. Amanda, watching from a corner of the room, swallowed hard. "Excuse me!" she said suddenly. She walked out and stood in the corridor. Where could one go and seek refuge in this big school? There was not a place beside the office she had just left. The empty classrooms were locked. Slowly she headed toward the bathroom, entered, and locked the door on herself. She prayed, "Oh Lord, I don't know what to do. Out of respect for You, I can't stay to watch that, even if it doesn't work. Show me please what to do."

She opened her eyes and waited for a few more minutes. Finally, her face relaxed. "Lord God, I know You're above all that, and there's nothing to fear."

She stepped out and went back to the supervisors' lounge. She breathed deeply, took hold of the doorknob, and entered. "Hi!" she exclaimed. "Watch it, boys, the glasses are flying!"

They turned toward her. She was smiling at them mischievously.

"You are distracting us!"

"Sorry, but there's no other place for me to go, and I'll never be able to sit quietly that long."

The boys glanced at each other. They understood. "All right. If we can't concentrate, it's useless to even try."

"Too bad. We'll try again another time."

"Preferably when I'm not around!" Amanda added.

They were not upset at her.

"By the way," she began again, "I'd be interested in a discussion with you about psychic control. What attracts you to that?"

They thought for a few seconds. "Power!" Manu said finally.

"Really?"

He nodded.

"I'm surprised you don't go to God instead, then. He is the Almighty."

"Maybe, but it's not the same."

"Manu, you're a friend. I'd be guilty not to warn you. Occultism is not innocent. God forbids it—and if He does, it's to protect us."

The boys listened carefully. "Maybe," Manu answered, "but I still want to try."

"Make sure you think it through before you go on," she insisted. Then she sighed. He seemed already hooked.

* * *

The next week, M. Villemin was back. When Amanda arrived, Véronique was finishing her session. She put her instrument away, and the two girls greeted each other.

"Mademoiselle Vissac!"

"Bonjour, monsieur!" she answered.

While she was placing a viola technique book on the music stand, he was observing her quietly. "Leave that, will you!"

She looked at him and waited.

"Play your sarabande for me."

She set the Suites de Bach on the stand and obeyed. M. Villemin interrupted his pupils only very rarely when they played, so she played the sarabande from the beginning to the end.

"Well!" he simply commented. He turned his back on her, as he usually did when he had a delicate question to ask. "Amanda, what happened last week with my substitute?"

She opened her mouth, blushed, but didn't answer.

"Tell me, I want an explanation!" he insisted severely.

"Well, he wanted me to play that piece faster than that."

"Then?"

"I didn't play faster."

"Why not?"

"Because I don't like it fast. I like this piece slow."

"Is that all?"

"Oui, monsieur."

He slowly turned back and stared at her. "Amanda, if you'd like, I'll take you to professionalism!"

She breathed again, her face brightened, her eyes shone.

"Like your friend Cédric!" he added.

AT THE HEALTH FOOD STORE

AMANDA WALKED TO SIMONE'S. WHEN she entered the health food store, Simone was filling a shelf with hazelnut-butter jars.

"Bonjour, Amanda."

"It's cool and quiet here," the young lady remarked.

"Yes, it's peaceful."

Amanda sniffed. "It smells good too!"

"What would you like?"

"Could you spare a minute? I'd like to talk to you."

Simone put the half-emptied box down on the floor and turned around. "I knew you were coming to talk to me."

"How did you know that?"

Simone was hesitant. "I don't know. Intuition, I suppose."

The two women stared at each other. Amanda started again. "Do you remember the last time we went to evangelize in the street? We asked people the question: 'Do you believe in God?' Most of the people didn't even want to answer. Others said they were atheists. Then, at one point, a man told me, 'I'm a Moslem!' I was so happy. I told him, 'You believe in God then!' Do you know what his answer was?"

Simone shrugged, meaning she didn't know.

"He said, 'No, I'm an atheist.' I said, 'But Moslems believe in God!' He answered me saying, 'I'm a Moslem and an atheist.'"

"People are strange!" Simone remarked.

"These last months, I've met many people with strange beliefs. I wonder how to explain the gospel to them. I realize I don't know my Bible well enough. In fact, what I'd really like to do is study the Bible. I'm wondering if there doesn't exist a place . . . somewhere . . . where I could do just that."

Simone was holding her breath. "Oh, Amanda!"

"Would you happen to have any information to guide me?"

"Listen! One of my friends is a teacher in one of the best French Bible schools. Come back tomorrow. I'll bring you the address."

"Wonderful! Thanks, Simone."

A customer entered. Amanda quickly told her friend, "Don't forget. I'll see you tomorrow."

She stepped into the warmth of the spring.

* * *

A few days later, at lunch time, Louise and Amanda were both sitting at the kitchen table, a steaming meal between the two of them.

"What are you going to do now that you have your driver's license?" her mother asked.

Amanda had just started on a chicken leg that she was holding with her fingers. "You'll soon be able to buy yourself a car," Louise continued, as she got up to get the salt.

The young lady glanced up at her mother. "You know, Maman," she began shyly, "I think I'll have enough money to start studying again."

"Studies? What kind of studies?" Surprised, Louise forgot to sit back.

"I'd like to study the Bible."

"Study the Bible?"

"Yes, what do you think of it?"

Against all expectations, her mother answered with an unusual harshness. "If you leave to study the Bible . . . I warn you, Amanda, you'll never step back into this house!"

Amanda slowly put the chicken leg back on her plate. She couldn't swallow anymore. She tried to hold her tears back—then finally got up to seek refuge in her room.

* * *

In the early afternoon, Simone's store was still empty of customers, and Amanda had just shared her latest news with her friend.

"This is strange," the woman remarked. "Why would your mother be opposed to you studying the Bible? She is a Christian, isn't she?"

"I don't know. I don't understand." Amanda sighed.

"And what about your father, what does he say about it?"

"He doesn't say anything. I think he's afraid to get in between the two of us."

"Well, what are you going to do then?"

"As long as I live with my parents, I consider they still have a say in my life. I won't go without their consent."

Simone sighed. "What a shame. However . . ." She bit her lip.

"Simone, I still have the conviction that the Lord is calling me to study His Word. If this is truly of Him, as I believe it is, He'll open the door. In any case, He'll have to open this one. Meanwhile, I have enough money for a first year of study."

"Good."

"Listen! I'm going to tell you something, for you alone. It's probably best that someone should know."

Simone was paying attention.

"The Easter break is approaching. I'm going to spend it in Sologne, at the house we've just inherited from my great-uncle. I'll be by myself for about ten days. I'm going to pray, fast, and spend some time with God."

"How long do you intend to fast?"

"Seven days, on water only."

"That's a lot. Do you know how to do it?"

Amanda smiled. "I've read one of your books. Don't worry."

"I won't worry, but I'll pray for you. Don't forget to drink a lot of water."

"Water is good over there."

The entry door opened. A customer stepped in.

"I must be going. Au revoir, Simone."

"Au revoir. Take care of yourself!"

Thoughtful, the shopkeeper went back behind her counter.

THE SONG OF THE NIGHTINGALE

IN THE HEART OF THE forests and ponds of the Sologne region, the small village of Boisvert had retained a picturesque aspect of more ancient times. The houses were made of red bricks, and the windows decorated with geraniums. On the outskirts, a century-old house was keeping watch over a country heritage. There, Amanda was starting her third day of fast. She read a chapter of the Gospel of John, then slowly drank a big glass of water and walked one kilometer to the village. At the post office, she briefly called her mother on the phone. "I'm doing fine."

"What did you say? I can barely hear you."

"I said I'm fine," Amanda repeated, hardly louder. Her voice was weakened by the fast. She slowly walked back home, entered the grassy yard, and passed by the shed to her right. The heavy cart of Mouton[26], her great-uncle's last draught-horse, was still parked there. Her great-uncle had been a lumberman, and Mouton had been his gentle, powerful companion.

---

[26]Sheep

That evening, Amanda went to bed early in her little attic bedroom and fell asleep. In the middle of the night, light noises woke her up with a start. She sat up, covered with cold sweat, and turned on the light. She remained sitting for a while without moving, listening intently. The noises had stopped, but fear had seized her. Finally, she took hold of the Bible that was by her side and opened it at random to find some comfort. She happened on the fourth Psalm and read aloud. She came to verse eight. "In peace I will both lie down and sleep, for You alone, O Lord, make me to dwell in safety.[27]"

She smiled, turned the light off, and went back to sleep. That night, she dreamed of a table covered with a delicious festival banquet, and she was eating . . . to the full.

* * *

Four days later, Amanda reached her seventh day of fasting. At the end of a soft spring day, she came to sit outside, next to the back entry door, in front of the garden. Not far from her, the little cherry tree was covered with glittering white blooms. She finished reading the whole Gospel of John.

Amanda was meditating when suddenly, dark clouds accumulated on the horizon. Lightning streaked the sky. Rolls of thunder rapidly approached, and heavy raindrops splattered the ground in front of her. She closed her Bible and found refuge in her room. Looking through the attic window from her bed, she enjoyed a splendid view of the storm that was raging outside. It was violent, but it stopped as quickly as it had started.

---

[27]The Scripture mentioned here is from the New American Standard Bible published by Zondervan.

Under a lighter wind, the trees shook their last drippings. Then, an extraordinary stillness settled in, as impressive as the preceding tumult. Waves of silence floated through the air. Amanda held her breath so as not to trouble this divine peace. Suddenly, from the midst of this prodigious atmosphere, a song of pure beauty arose toward the heavens. The eyes of the girl filled with tears. A nightingale had found refuge under the eaves of the barn. He sang late into the night.

⋆ ⋆ ⋆

Two months later at the Conservatoire de Versailles, Amanda entered the room for her oral test in music theory. Two middle-aged ladies were administering it. One of them put a sheet of music paper on the stand. Amanda read the few measures written in the treble clef without any problem. The examiner added another sheet to the first one. More slowly by now, the girl read off the notes in the bass clef. The lady then placed a music sheet in the D clef on top of the others. The student read these notes very slowly.

"Hmm," declared the lady. "This is not too good. Let's try the C clef."

Amanda read with a lot of stops and starts. The woman interrupted her before she was finished. "Tell me, young lady, according to the information we have here right under our eyes, you are a violist, aren't you?"

"Yes, I am."

"Violists play in the C clef, don't they? If I make no mistake, this is the clef you work with, isn't it?"

"Yes, it is."

"And you can't read even it!" She shook her head with disapproval and went on. "It seems to me you've already taken your instrumental exams, which included practical sight-reading."

"Yes, madame, I have."

"Let me check on your results!" She pulled a folder from a metal file cabinet and sat down beside her colleague. "Well now!" she exclaimed. "This is unbelievable! You have excellent marks and a top level in sight-reading. How did you do that? Could you explain this mystery to me?"

"Well, yes . . . of course!"

"All right, I'm listening to you, mademoiselle!" the lady said sharply.

"Well . . . I read the notes with my fingers."

Amanda was very serious, but she couldn't help exuding a spark of victory with her eyes. That was enough to set fire to the gunpowder of the examiner's reaction.

The examiner arose. "Mademoiselle Vissac, at this level you are supposed to know five clefs, and by the end of next year, it should be the entire seven. I'm stipulating that your instrumental first medal be withheld from you this year. This will teach you a lesson! You may leave."

Without a word, the young musician left the room.

* * *

At the beginning of July, the Vissac family arrived at Boisvert, in Sologne, to spend their summer vacation. Louise's parents had preceded them from Belfort. The country house had enough rooms to shelter everyone. In the kitchen, Mémère and Louise were preparing lunch while Armand kept them company, picking fresh garden peas from their pods. In the barn, Pépère was fixing a door. Amanda, standing with her back leaning against the red brick wall between the door and the window, could hear the hammerings. Hands buried in the pockets of her shorts, she was gazing at the century-old walnut tree. Only a few meters from her, it cast its generous shadow on a good part of the yard where the grass still grew a luxuriant green. Birds were pursuing each other in its branches. Swallows that had established their residence under the barn's eaves were hovering above the tall tree and catching all kinds of winged insects.

The hammerings stopped; Pépère came out of the barn. A smile of satisfaction on his lips, he headed toward the house and his granddaughter. "That's it. I'm done!"

Amanda smiled back at him. "You did a nice job, Pépère!"

He stopped in front of her. "And what about you, mon petit[28]? What do you intend to do later with your life?"

She shrugged. "I don't know . . ."

"All the same, at your age, you should have an idea!"

"Maybe, but who cares? It's useless."

"What do you mean, it's useless?"

She told him, "The only thing I'd like to do, I can't; so it's better not to talk about it."

Pépère observed her silently. "Well, tell me!" he insisted gently. "I'd still like to know."

She sighed. "If I could, I would like to study the Bible."

Pépère took one step back. He was moved. "If I could start my life again, this is what I would do," he pronounced softly.

---

[28]My little one: Pépère used this expression in the masculine form, in an affectionate way.

Amanda opened her mouth with surprise. “Oh Pépère! Really?”

“Really! However, I can’t start my life over again. But tell me, what keeps you from pursuing this?”

The face of his granddaughter became sullen. “Maman doesn’t agree, and I believe, as a Christian, I shouldn’t go against her will as long as I’m living under her roof.”

“Listen,” he ordered, “don’t move from here! I’m going in to talk to your parents, right now.”

Without another word, Pépère stepped inside the kitchen. The door closed on him.

This book is missing the last chapters!

EPILOGUE

CÉDRIC (NOT HIS REAL NAME), the violist, entered the Conservatoire National Supérieur de Paris after studying at the Conservatoire National Supérieur de Lyon. Then he went on to a foreign country where he obtained a medal of merit. Back in France, he became employed in a renowned orchestra, as solo violist.

ANNEX

AMANDA'S COMPLETE PRESENTATION ABOUT DEATH, in philosophy class, in twelfth grade:

DEATH.

I. LIFE AND DEATH

A. The Death of the Universe

DEATH CAN BE PRESENTED AS a very general physical phenomenon which is not specific to the living being but which concerns, in a larger sense, any closed system. The thermal death of the universe is explained scientifically by the Second Law of Thermodynamics. Because all forms of energy transform naturally into heat, and because the intensity of that heat tends naturally toward its lowest level, the universe, being physically a closed system—unable to obtain energy from another source—will, after a finite period of time, reach a point of maximum entropy—absolute disorder! That is, it will become a dead universe.

B. The Mystery of Life

There is one exception to this Second Law of Thermodynamics: the living being who before dying has developed fully and reproduced itself. The history of life is one of "a growth of information," while the law of entropy in the material world is a law of de-information, a law of death. During the 19th century, Bichat wrote, "Life is a combination of forces, which resist death."

Thanatocracy is a term meaning the absolute and ultimate power of death. This is the point of view promoted by the nihilist philosophers. Other philosophers voice reservations about thanatocracy: Is the universe a closed, limited system? Nothing allows us to assert that; but nothing allows us to deny, either, the possible presence of life in other parts of the universe. If the universe is not seen as a physically closed system, we must admit that it receives, in a continuous manner, some creative information. The idea of a creative evolution implies a source of life. We can call the source of this information God.

C. The True Problem of Death

THE CONCEPT OF DEATH OF the universe has merely a vague significance. Death—in the strict significance of the term—concerns only living beings. It is the transformation of a living organism into a dead body. However, the problem of death is truly only important to man. Actually, the crossing from nature to culture, which defines humanity, is manifested not only by the invention of tools and by a complex language but also by the acknowledgement of death and the institution of burial places, which we don't find in the animal world according to historical proofs. Certainly, all the care given to the corpse manifests more a hope in immortality than an affirmation of death. All civilizations have affirmed the immortality of people. Edgar Morin said, "The same conscience denies and acknowledges death. It denies it as an utter destruction and recognizes it as an event."

II. PHILOSOPHY, A MEDITATION ON LIFE AND DEATH

A. Philosophy, a Meditation on Life

SHOULD THE PHILOSOPHER MEDITATE ON life or meditate on death? The opinions are divergent. Plato (Phédon) said, "To philosophize is to learn to die." Socrates' death is an example. Spinoza affirms that "the true philosopher never thinks about death and that his wisdom is not a meditation about death but about life" (Ethics, book IV, prop. 617) and also in his Traité Politique, V, chap. 6: "While one is only trying to avoid death, the other one is trying to do something with his life." With Spinoza the thought of death is contradictory, for pretending to think about "nothing" is the equivalent of thinking nothing. Plato and Spinoza, with opposing formulas, are saying the same thing: "Man, as a thinking being—as a being that knows true ideas—participates in the eternity of these ideas and escapes his apparent mortal condition."

B. Philosophy Can't Forget Death

1. Platonic or Spinozist, the philosophy of eternal ideas, which claims to meditate only on the true life, rests on a confusion

between the true Idea, eternal and indestructible, and the ephemeral I. Our fragile being remains the support of all of our thoughts. Mr. Jankélévitch said: "The thought doesn't kill death, but it is death that kills the thought."

2. For the materialist philosophers (Epicure, Lucrece) who don't believe in eternal ideas, nor in the immortality of people, it is however not appropriate to worry one second about death. Death and I can never meet.

"How can't we see that in real death there won't be any other me who, remained alive, will be able to lament my own loss?" ~ Lucrece

"After death, everything ends, even death." ~ Seneca

Death doesn't concern us, neither dead nor alive. "Nor alive" because, at that point, it doesn't exist; "neither dead" because, at that point, we are no more.

3. We can look at death from different angles: one dies, you die, I'm going to die.

a.) Death in the third person.

IT IS ABSTRACT AND ANONYMOUS. It is at the same time the death of everybody and the death of nobody. It is even common and daily. To speak of death in the third person, to say "one still dies from hunger in under-developed countries," is to treat death like a speech subject. It is to betray its true significance.

b.) The question of death is very different when it is asked in the second person. It is not a question anymore of this conceptual monster of impersonal death (one dies) but is a tragic experience, the experience of the death of another, and not just "any" other but of the one to whom I talk in the second person, whom I love with friendship, affection, or love.

c.) Is death in the first person—my own death—really a wrong problem?

HERE IS THE DEATH IN the third person: he died, he is dying, and he will die.

Here is the death in the second person: you are dying and you will die.

If it is impossible to say "I am dead," then "I am dying" remains unsure. But it is perfectly possible to say "I will die." It is even a certainty.

As long as the time is unknown to me, I can neglect to think about my death. But to say that death doesn't concern me is to deny a fact—to forget the consciousness of time.

Heidegger said, "As soon as a man is born, he is old enough to die."

Philosophy can't escape the meditation on death. The truth is that death is for each one of us a personal business.

C. Philosophy, Meditation on Life and Death

THE OPPOSITE PHILOSOPHIES, WHICH WE have examined so far, have a common postulate, which consists of opposing the thought of life and the thought of death in radical ways. However, we can adopt a philosophical attitude according to which meditation on life and meditation on death, instead of excluding each other, find their meaning only one with the other.

First of all, the thought of death wouldn't prevent the philosopher from living and living well. In a certain way, death itself gives life its very meaning. This is true in a scientific way. The characteristic of the most evolved living beings is that they are mortal. At the existential level itself, the thought of death and the thought of life are complementary. Life alone gives to the thought of death its tragic character. Death alone makes us think of life as being precious and fragile. Finally, life has significance and is precious because we dispose only of a limited time, and are therefore able to be organized.

The meditation on death is necessary. It helps us understand the value of life. Can we then find some philosophic serenity, affirm that death gives life its significance by putting an end to it? This doesn't bring any solution to the mortal condition of man. Is there a solution? It seems that the answer of philosophy is no. (Class book).

III. DOES RELIGION GIVE A SOLUTION?

HOWEVER, HISTORY GIVES US ANOTHER point of view. Man didn't need philosophy to start asking questions about death. What are his answers? They belong to the sacred and lead us inevitably to the religious domain.

Religions contain different doctrines and ways of coping. Religions offer ways to reach heaven, starting from the earth. Coming from man, no one can pretend with assurance to hold the truth. However, there is one exception, which came down from heaven to earth—from God to man. This religion, different from the others in its very nature, is the revelation of the good news in the person of Jesus Christ. The founders of the other great religions presented themselves as mere human beings and thought of themselves that way. Buddha said at the end of his life, "I'm still searching for the truth."

Christ, according to his own claim, is Son of God and said, "I am the truth." If we want to find answers to our questions—"Why death? Why are we born to die?"—the best way is to turn to Christianity and to the Bible. The Bible takes us back to the creation. The beginning of man is recorded in the three first chapters of Genesis, the first book of the Bible.[29]

In Genesis chapter one, death is not spoken of yet. Everything is beautiful and good for man.

However, Ecclesiastes 7:29 tells us, "Behold, I have found only this, that God made men upright, but they have sought out many devices."

In Genesis chapter two, God warns man of a danger. For the first time in the Bible, we find the mention of death. God also grants man full freedom of choice between life and death.

In Genesis chapter three, in the Garden of Eden, Adam's choice is called sin. It is the cause of death.

Romans 5:12. "Therefore, just as through one man sin entered into the world, and death through sin, and so death spread to all men, because all sinned . . ."

---

[29]The Scriptures mentioned here are taken from the New American Standard Bible published by Zondervan.

In the Bible, God defines sin in the Ten Commandments and in other laws.

James 4:17. "Therefore, to one who knows the right thing to do and does not do it, to him it is sin."

1 John 3:4. "Everyone who practices sin also practices lawlessness; and sin is lawlessness."

Is every man a sinner?

Genesis 8:21. "The Lord said to Himself, 'I will never again curse the ground on account of man, for the intent of man's heart is evil from his youth.'"

Psalm 14:1. "The fool has said in his heart, 'There is no God.'"

Proverbs 20:9. "Who can say, 'I have cleansed my heart, I am pure from my sin'?"

Ecclesiastes 7:20. "Indeed, there is not a righteous man on earth who continually does good and who never sins."

Isaiah 64:7. "There is no one who calls on Your name, who arouses himself to take hold of You; for You have hidden Your face from us, and have delivered us into the power of our iniquities."

The Bible doesn't only convince us of sin and therefore of death. It also gives us a solution to death.

Romans 6:23. "For the wages of sin is death, but the free gift of God is eternal life in Christ Jesus our Lord."

The story of Amanda is true.

You can read the beginning of her story in

Silo Country, *which was published in March 2013.*

Coming soon!

CROSSROAD OF THE NATIONS

THE TRILOGY CONTINUES WITH THE story of Amanda's Bible school experiences. Amanda leaves La Serpe to go study at the Bible school in the Parisian suburb. Some call it the cocoon, the bubble, or another planet. For Amanda, the Bible school offers not only the opportunity to study theology and world religions; it offers also a unique occasion to discover a concentrate of nations and cultures. As she befriends Malika, the North-African girl; Stefan, the German boy; and many others, new challenges arise.

For more information about
Amanda Robin Larcher
&
The Song of the Viola
please visit:

www.AmandaRobinLarcher.blogspot.com
larcherobin@gmail.com
facebook.com/amanda.robinlarcher

For more information about
AMBASSADOR INTERNATIONAL
please visit:

www.ambassador-international.com
@AmbassadorIntl
www.facebook.com/AmbassadorIntl